PERSONAL
VALUING

PERSONAL VALUING

AN INTRODUCTION

Dale D. Simmons

NELSON-HALL nh CHICAGO

LIBRARY OF CONGRESS CATALOGING IN PUBLICATION DATA

Simmons, Dale D.
  Personal valuing.

  Bibliography: p.
  Includes index.
  1. Values. 2. Personality. I. Title.
BF778.S55   155.2   82-2191
ISBN 0-88229-565-9   AACR2

Manufactured in the United States of America

10   9   8   7   6   5   4   3   2   1

The paper in this book is pH neutral (acid-free).

CONTENTS

PREFACE

The riots, demonstrations, and other forms of civil disobedience that occurred in the United States during the 1960s and 1970s left a variety of lingering effects, some constructive and some not. One effect has been an explosion of new materials for what is called "values education." This development seems due to the awakened recognition that the mainstream value system that had guided the design of contemporary social institutions in America was but one of many alternative value systems treasured by American citizens. Educators, in turn, were faced with the recognition that their task was not to promote mainstream values but to develop those valuers placed in their care. In response, they turned to materials being promoted by their publishers as teaching packages in values education.

The next problem, then, is how to evaluate these teaching packages. No universally accepted theory or model of personal valuing exists upon which to base an evaluation of materials for values education. Each of us faces the possibility that our world does not know how to prove beyond a doubt what are the truly good values. We must also deal with the further realization that even scholars who study personal valuing cannot agree upon its exact nature. The current state of affairs seems to be that we have a variety of social institutions, some venerable and some fairly new, each promoting certain values, while we also have a variety of scholarly approaches to the nature of personal values, each promoting certain ideas and notions. No agreed-upon criteria have been established for what constitutes a complete set of human values, nor are there criteria for determining the completeness of any theory or model of valuing.

Thus we are thrown back on our own resources to choose the values that are best, not knowing the criteria by which to judge the quality of such choices. Similarly the scholar must choose the model of personal valuing that is most correct, without firm criteria by which to judge the correctness of the choice.

Any book, such as this one, written as a primer about the various scholarly research approaches to human valuing will automatically reflect the author's bias and will be judged variously poor, fair, or worthwhile according to the criteria selected by the judges. Let us begin then with this bias. The author believes that values are those of our beliefs that define for us the nature of the Good Life, the good ways to behave and to be. We organize our values into systems on an individual level, with each person's value system being uniquely organized. These systems are dynamic, being continuously reorganized. We incorporate values into the system while we discard old ones and revise priorities. Dynamic changes in our value systems occur in response to internal conflicts as well as to external pressures. Our values provide us with guidelines for interpreting the significance of life events, with the foundations for establishing interpersonal ties and group membership, and with the directions necessary for the construction of a life pathway. We are free to choose those values that will serve us as guides through the increasingly complex set of circumstances we call daily life; we are not free from circumstances, yet we are free to choose how we will deal with those circumstances.

This book is a primer directed to three audiences: (1) the general reader or student interested in what the contemporary social scientist has to say about human valuing; (2) the educator interested in some sort of "road map" through the realm of values education; and (3) the professional psychologist who recognizes that values are central to any understanding of an individual, yet whose professional training has left a huge emptiness about valuing because "psychology is value-free and does not deal with such matters."

This book is about modern views of valuing, not the classical philosophical views, and deals with the empirically directed notions of social
science rather than the discussion-centered notions of the philosophers.
The theorists to be reviewed are those whose ideas have resulted in the
generation of some sort of procedure for gathering empirical data about
the valuing of the individual person. Many discussions that have not led
to research procedures are worthy; they are, however, simply not the
concern of this book.

In the first chapter a model is proposed, in personalized form, for
understanding the main facets of valuing. The introduction of two
young persons as valuers allows the distinction between value content,
value fulfillment, and valuing competence to be clarified. The second
chapter provides an introduction to the emerging field of axiology (the
study of valuing) and reviews the more significant scholars' perspectives
on human valuing. Because the only scholars to be reviewed are those
whose ideas have resulted in devices for assessing the valuing of individuals, the reader can assume that a central portion of the research on
human valuing has derived from the writings of these scholars.

Each of the next three chapters focuses upon one of the three facets
of valuing. The third chapter examines the content and structure of
value systems, primarily as research findings have reflected upon theoretical models. Particular attention is given to the various attempts to
"factor out" statistically *the* basic underlying dimensions of value systems. (Because this is an introductory book, however, the review of the
research is illustrative rather than comprehensive.) The reader will have
an opportunity to consider the notion that each of us has a few major
values, around which are clustered the multitude of specific values
appearing in daily life.

The fulfillment of our values, the satisfactions arising out of our
hopes and fears, and the actualization of our potential and our goals are
the central topics in the fourth chapter. This chapter specifically notes
the emergence of research into the quality of life, which I predict will
become a major field of study in the future. The fifth chapter reviews
the major attempts to understand the basic skills in making good value
choices and correct value judgments. Is anything involved in being a

competent valuer beyond using proper logic? Will correct value judgment lead to the selection of certain values as the best?

At the end of each of these three chapters, i.e., three, four, and five, I have felt free to add my own ideas, derived from several years of work with an approach to valuing referred to as Values Exploration.

In addition to these remarks, some of which are a rejoinder to the material presented in the main body of each chapter, the ideas presented in chapter six are further expressions of my own point of view. The concept of "axiological maturity" is proposed as a means of linking and resynthesizing the three facets of valuing (content, fulfillment, and competence), which have been isolated for the purpose of exposition. This chapter also provides a "mini-workshop," a chance for you, the reader, to examine your own valuing, to sort out your own values, to identify how your values are expressed in your behavior, and to plan some new expressions for some of your important values which you have been slighting.

The ideas reviewed in this book are not just about valuing; they are about *your* valuing. Hence, the last part of this book is devoted to giving you a chance to compare "the menu with the meal." (You might want to begin with the mini-workshop and to read about the scholars' ideas on valuing only after you have examined your own valuing. If so, you should turn first to the section in the last chapter entitled "Personal Development: Choosing, Expressing, and Planning.")

I have a "fantasy critic" who disclaims any real merit in this book because it is "just linear thought applied to the nature of virtue, . . . a book about the modern drums being beaten during the search for the fugitive, value." You, the reader, will have to decide whether you have caught a glimpse of this fugitive while spending time with this book.

I can only acknowledge with gratitude the willingness of the hundreds of persons who, as students and instructors at Oregon State University, openly shared their valuing so that I might think about valuing as recorded in this book. And, a final thank you to Mrs. Louise Garrison, of the Department of English at O.S.U., whose thorough editorial comments stimulated extensive improvements in the writing of the text.

1.

Saralynn and Gregg

LET US CREATE A FICTION, portraits of two young persons as valuers. Saralynn and Gregg are the same age and from similar social backgrounds. They seem normal in outlook and are physically healthy, without any known situational crises at present. Both are personable, cooperative, pleasant in appearance, and typical in attire.

I ask Saralynn, "What are your personal values?"

She thinks a while before she says, "Well . . . uh . . . I guess I have a lot of values. I value my family, our close relationships. I value my friendships. I value the sunsets and everything beautiful. I value my activities, how I spend my time. I value telling the truth and being myself. I value being healthy and not sick. I value being outdoors and riding horses." Saralynn asks me if I have a horse. When I say "No," she says "Oh." She then continues, "I value being able to do things for myself, cooking, sewing, driving, and all the things that help you be independent and free. I value liberty and our country and the rights we have."

She pauses for a while, then says rather seriously, "I seem to be changing. It's just something that's happening to me. I love all my family and friends, but I find I'm valuing my privacy more than before. I find myself sitting looking out the window thinking about things, and I value my thoughts. I'm not daydreaming; I don't value that. I'm thinking some things through—you know what I mean. I've joined a mountain-climbing group. It doesn't mean I don't value my health, but

I just wonder if I have the guts to do something really risky and adventurous.

"And I don't always tell my friends how I feel anymore. I don't know, I guess I'm afraid that the truth would hurt them or they wouldn't really understand me. I expect them to say to me, 'Who do you think you're trying to kid?' I value being diplomatic a lot more than I used to. I guess I must sound mixed-up to you?" Saralynn looks at me inquiringly.

I ask Gregg, "What are your personal values?"

He says immediately, "I value working, and doing everything as good as I can. If I can't do something as good as I want to, I just won't do it, so I almost always do a good job of everything I do. I value taking care of myself, which I do. I take good care of my car and help out the kids in the family. I value the sports which I'm good at. You know, when I think about it, it seems these have always been my values for as long as I can remember."

"Saralynn, how fulfilled are your values?" I ask.

"Gee, if you'd only asked me that a year ago, I'd have said, without question, 'very'. But now, like I said, I'm changing, and some of my values are not being fulfilled. Some of them are, you know, but some of them I'm not even sure how they could be fulfilled. I seem to be moody, but I'm not really. It's just that from minute to minute one value is being satisfied, and then I realize that another one is being ignored and I don't know what to do about it."

Turning back to Gregg, I decide not to ask him, "How fulfilled are your values?" because he has already made it clear that he limits himself to that which he can do "good." I ask instead, "When an important value of yours comes into conflict with the values of another person, what do you do?"

He says, "I'm always polite, but nobody is going to force their values on me. I usually get out of the situation as quick as I can. There's no use to just arguing and hassling and fighting when neither of you will give in."

Saralynn, when asked the same question, says quickly, "Oh, I like to get the other person to sit and talk with me about it. First, you have to establish something in common, something you both share and care about, so even if you get mad at each other you remember that there's more to your relationship than this one 'mad-thing.' Next, I try to find out what the other person is really thinking about. I want them to know I care about what they are thinking. If I don't think they'll get the wrong idea, I may even touch them, too, just to let them know in another way that I care about us. Then, I try to figure out whether we really do have a value conflict or whether we just think we do. I mean, I find out sometimes you really agree, but just the way you talk about it makes you think you don't agree. I try to figure out whether the value is extremely important for them or for me. If it's really important to the other person but only so-so for me, I'm usually ready to compromise and go along with them. But that's only if I can't figure out some way we can do something so that both of us can have our ways. And that's not as hard as some people think. I consider whether we can make a deal or trade. Today I'll go along with you if you'll go along with me tomorrow. Oh, there's lots of things to do when you have a conflict, to work it out, you know. But you have to have one before you know which way to go. I mean each one is so different."

These portraits of Saralynn and Gregg are presented to illustrate the three main aspects of personal valuing, the three ways we can look at valuers. We differ among ourselves in what we value (*content*), we differ in how fulfilled we are as valuers (*actualization*), and we differ among ourselves in our effectiveness as valuers (*competence*). To gain insight into these three realms, we can begin with three questions: "What are your personal values?" "How fulfilled are your values?" and "When an important value of yours comes into conflict with the values of another person, what do you do?"

Saralynn's and Gregg's responses illustrate readily these three dimensions of valuing. Focusing on *content*, we find Saralynn to have an extended range of values, and we find her in a period of transition in content. What she values seems clear, both in her older, basic values and in her newer ones. Her older values are primarily social and aesthetic ones (in the classical sense), with a valuing of autonomy added. Her newer values center around an increased appreciation of inner experience (including the experiencing of vital excitement) and an increased valuing of a controlled, but a kindly, style of interacting with others.

Gregg, on the other hand, does not appear to have an extended range of values content. His primary value is effectiveness in action, and he seems to seek this in all experience. To him it is a cardinal value. Unlike Saralynn, Gregg appears to have stable, firm, value content.

When it comes to *actualization*, we must consider Gregg almost completely fulfilled. Partially he is so because he is careful not to undertake anything that might lead to questions about his effectiveness in action. Saralynn, in some contrast, is only partially (or better stated, episodically) actualized. She is satisfied one moment, not satisfied the next. We can attribute part of this incomplete fulfillment to the growth process, to the development of new values that have not yet been graced with automatic satisfiers. Even so, Saralynn cannot be judged to be as fulfilled, satisfied, and actualized as Gregg.

While Gregg's value system may seem stable and fulfilled, and while Saralynn's may seem changing and only partially fulfilled, we find a rather different perspective on these two valuers when we examine them from the point of view of *competence*. Gregg reveals little adaptive flexibility in coping with value conflict (a central dynamic in the growth and effectiveness of a value system). When faced with an interpersonal value conflict, he seems to put on a "character armor" and just walks away, his main concern being to protect his values from challenge.

Saralynn is remarkably more competent. She has a pattern for coping. She "sets the scene" for problem solving before she even begins to deal with the value conflict. She considers the relative importance of the values to each of the persons involved. Whether Saralynn was taught her competency or whether she just worked it out independently while solving problems with which she was faced is a secondary matter. The primary matter here is that she is clearly very competent to deal with interpersonal value conflicts, more so than Gregg.

On the basis of just three questions we can now draw surprisingly clear portraits of two young people as valuers. Gregg values effectiveness in action and feels fulfilled because he limits his efforts to activities in which he will prove effective; but despite his concern for effectiveness, he is not a very competent valuer because he reveals few skills for dealing with interpersonal value conflicts. Saralynn has a wide range of values, mostly social and aesthetic, which reveal developmental changes. She is less fulfilled because of these changes but is a most competent valuer whose skills suggest a rich future for her in valuing.

Summary

Through a consideration of the valuing processes of Saralynn and of Gregg, three facets of valuing have been described. The first facet is the content of value systems, the second is the degree to which values and the valuer are fulfilled or actualized, and the third is the competency of the valuer.

2.

Scholarly Views
on Valuing

PHILOSOPHERS, SOCIAL SCIENTISTS, and mental health specialists have regularly concerned themselves with valuing. Unfortunately for us, each scholar or writer has tended to focus on one of the three facets of valuing. As a result, we do not find ourselves with a common core of understandings about human valuing; we do not find an agreed-upon list of principles describing the nature of valuing.

Those who concern themselves with values are now called *axiologists – axios* being the Greek word for "worth." When we read the axiological literature, we must look hard for even a common set of topics or themes. It is as if a whole group of axiologically oriented scholars were wandering around in the dark with lamps, searching for the essence of valuing; yet the searchers were so separated that one scholar rarely noticed another's illumination. Some have concerned themselves with the content of value systems, some with the fulfillment of values and valuers, and others with competence to value.

Before any review of the ideas that particular scholars have developed concerning the nature of human valuing, a clarification must be made. According to Sahakian (1968) in his *Systems of Ethics and Value Theory*, ethics is *the study of right conduct and the good life*. Some philosophers, however, are more restrictive and limit ethics to the study of right and wrong conduct, of the moral and the immoral. Others emphasize ethics as the study of the form of life that is most worthy. Those

7

who restrict themselves to the study of obligatory conduct are referred to as *deontologists*, while those who restrict themselves to the study of goodness and the good life are referred to as *axiologists*. Other philosophers argue that the Right and the Good are intertwined, complementary, essentially indistinguishable. To these scholars the distinction is primarily an academic, or an arbitrary, one. The main points here are that philosophers place the study of valuing in the field of ethics and apply the term *axiologist* to those who concern themselves with the nature of valuing.

Axiology is a relatively new, emerging branch of inquiry, with only a short history of professional concern (Hartman, 1967; Findlay, 1970). Because the Good, and the good life, are matters of daily attention to many people besides philosophers, it is not surprising that scholars in many other fields have discussed such things. Though these writers may originally have been psychologists, educators, anthropologists, psychiatrists, etc., their concern with personal valuing has made them axiologists also.

Much of the confusion in axiology as a field derives from the inclination of scholars to approach valuing from the vantage point of their own professional specialty. Rarely have the writers "searched the literature" in other disciplines before they expressed their ideas. Hence, the description of valuing by such scholars is analogous to the proverbial description of the elephant by a group of blind men, each of whom has touched only part of the elephant and then assumed that part defined the whole beast.

The scholars whose writings have been of most interest to your author and, in his judgment, the most advanced are those whose ideas have produced a procedure for inventorying the personal valuing of an individual. Though the ideas of some writers seem appealing and rational, their true merits cannot be evaluated until they can be applied to an instance. Hence, we will review only those writers whose ideas have resulted in a method of assessment that has been used in research.

The division of scholarly writing into three classifications—content, fulfillment, and competence—offers some promise of categorizing and relating the ideas of axiologically oriented writers. A truly comprehensive value theory, covering all three facets, is not available. At this point, we will be examining a series of one-facet theories, a few of which attend to a second facet. Each approach to valuing will be presented somewhat uncritically, as a "thumbnail sketch" of the key concepts of the writer. Our purpose is to provide an intellectual framework for understanding axiology, as represented by a selected set of authors whose ideas have been put into practice, rather than to present a critically analyzed assessment of the merits of the proposals made by each author.

APPROACHES EMPHASIZING CONTENT AND STRUCTURE

Eduard Spranger, a German developmental psychologist writing in the 1920s, proposed that value systems are constructed out of, or on the basis of, six *valuing attitudes:* economic, aesthetic, theoretic, political, social, and religious. These valuing attitudes arise in part from the levels of the self (the biological, the perceptual, the rational, and the spiritual), and in part from the social environment (interpersonal ties and sociopolitical structures). For any individual, these values are organized into priority systems, and this organization in turn influences how an individual perceives and evaluates his life situation. For example, a person with a dominant theoretic orientation with secondary economic and social valuing attitudes might tend to focus upon a rational analysis of the role of economics on social relationships.

Even though Spranger's book was titled *Types of Men* (1928), he was attempting to challenge the tendency at that time to classify people according to race or national origin. He hoped to substitute a psychological basis to explain the differences among humans. Spranger's goal was to specify the values that, when combined by an individual, would produce a unique value pattern. His model of the six valuing attitudes led Philip Vernon and Gordon Allport (1931) to create the Study of Values, a research instrument that for the next thirty years was the most widely used measure of personal values. Consequently, much of the empirical data currently available on personal valuing consists of scores on the Study of Values.

Charles Morris, an American semanticist and philosopher, proposed (1942, 1948, 1956) that the major religio-philosophical systems are based on a rank-ordering of three ways of satisfying human needs, namely, giving in to impulses, controlling impulses, and remaking the world. The rank orderings of these three tendencies produce value systems—total, integrated paths of life—that, when rationalized, become religio-philosophical systems.

The seven basic Paths of Life described by Morris were the Apollonian (preserving the best man has attained), the Buddhist (cultivating independence of persons and things), the Christian (showing sympathetic concern for others), the Dionysian (experiencing festivity and solitude in alternation), the Maitreyan (integrating action, contemplation, and enjoyment), the Mohammedan (acting and enjoying life through group participation), and the Promethean (constantly mastering changing conditions). From the cornerstones of enjoyment, assertive reconstruction of the world, and self-control come the varieties of human values.

Morris, in an effort to study the paths of life empirically, created a measuring device he named the Ways to Live Document. This instrument was originally limited to the seven paths, but was ultimately expanded to thirteen Ways. The Ways to Live Document has found its most extensive research use in cross-national comparisons of value patterns, providing, interestingly enough, the only empirical data known to the author on the values of mainland Chinese university students in the late 1940s, data gathered just before the shift to the Communist government and life pattern.

Florence Kluckhohn and Fred Strodtbeck, American anthropologists, proposed (1961) that the structure of social communities is based on "value orientations," which in turn consist of the solutions to five common human problems. Every community, and every person, faces the same set of problems, and each has available the same set of solutions to each problem. The differences between social communities and among persons reside in the rank-ordering of these available solutions to the common problems in human living, that is, in the value orientations. The problems facing us (with their alternative solutions) are (1) What is the basic nature of man? (good, evil, mixed, neither); (2) What will be man's relationship to nature? (subjugation to, harmony with, mastery over); (3) What is the preferred focus in time? (past, present, future); (4) What will be the orientation toward activity? (doing, being, being-in-becoming); and (5) What will be man's relationship to man? (lineal, collateral, individualistic).

Each social community will not only have a dominant value orientation but will also have variant value orientations which are not only tolerated but essential to the community. The dominant (middle-class, mainstream) American value orientation considers the basic nature of the human to be a mixture of good and evil, emphasizes human mastery over the environment, gives precedence to planning and living for the future, concentrates on accomplishments (doing), and affirms individualism in the relationship of humans to each other. A variant value orientation, identified by Papajohn and Speigel (1975) as the value orientation underlying many new forms of counseling and psychotherapy, considers basic human nature to be good, emphasizes the need for humans to live in harmony with their environment, gives precedence to living in the present and experiencing the here and now, concentrates upon being (rather than doing), and affirms collaterality as the correct basis for human relationships. On the basis of such value orientations, such solutions to common human problems, we construct patterns of daily living.

The Interview Schedule, designed by Kluckhohn and Strodtbeck as a tool for studying the value orientations of five distinctive cultural groups located in close proximity to one another, presents problem situations that allow respondents to reveal their preferred solutions to the common human problems. Because the schedule was designed for use with groups without a written language, it is administered orally. This procedure not only allows respondents to make known their choices but also provides an opportunity for qualification of preferences.

Milton Rokeach, a contemporary American social psychologist, has proposed (1973) that every person's value system consists of a rank-ordering of a set of terminal values (*end-states*) and a rank-ordering of a set of instrumental values (*means*). The terminal values are of two types, the *personal* (e.g., salvation, inner harmony) and the *social* (e.g., world peace, equality). There are also two types of instrumental values, the *moral* (e.g., being honest, being responsible) and the *competence* values (e.g., being logical, being imaginative). There are more instrumental values for people to choose among than terminal values. Rokeach also believes that social institutions are created by humans as a technique for maintaining, enhancing, and transmitting subsets of values.

Rokeach, as an experimental psychologist, was concerned with the ways a person resolves conflicts between his or her behavior and values. He was especially concerned with equality as a value and its role in civil-rights-oriented behavior. To facilitate his research, he created the Value Survey, consisting of a set of eighteen terminal values and a set of eighteen instrumental values. A subject was instructed to rank-order the values in each set from most to least important. In 1968 this Value Survey was used to measure the values of a representative sample of the American citizenry; the results remain the only such sampling available. At that time the highest ranked terminal values among U.S. citizens were "a world at peace," "family security," and "freedom," while the lowest ranked were "an exciting life," "pleasure," and "social recognition." The highest ranked instrumental values were being "honest," "responsible," and "ambitious" (for males) or "forgiving" (for females), while the lowest ranked were being "imaginative," logical," and "obedient."

William Eckhardt, the director of the Canadian Peace Research Institute, has gone beyond a description of the structure of value systems to the promotion of a specific set of values that he feels will enhance peace among men (Eckhardt, 1972). He has proposed that *compassion* be made the central, organizing, normative value, as the source from which humans can be helped to live in peace, honesty, and cooperation. Compassion, as defined by Eckhardt, consists of a set of values that includes a "radical faith" in human nature, altruism, creativity, and justice defined as equality. The opposite of compassion is compulsion, a set of disvalues—a negation of freedom and equality as values, which leads to social systems that restrict humans and produce social and intergroup conflict. The proper values, the values of compassion, may help to prevent humans from destroying themselves as a species.

The Compassion-Compulsion Scale, developed by Eckhardt for his research, consists of a series of statements with which a person may agree or disagree. The statements are in fact beliefs that are consistent with either compassionate values or compulsive values. One's value system is thus assessed through the beliefs that derive from one's basic position regarding compassion.

The above five perspectives on the value domain are obviously quite diverse. Each of us intuitively perceives every value to have merits; yet no one perspective appears to provide us with an overall coordinating structure of values that comprehends or anticipates all the different proposals. We do not, in fact, even have a set of criteria that would allow us to judge the comprehensiveness or the generality of any given proposed value structure. Rather, each scholar proceeds to describe the organization of his or her own ideal value system and proposes that this ideal structure be considered the general form. In the value domain, we only have a set of alternative proposals whose worth we cannot judge until some ultimate criteria for evaluation are proposed and accepted.

APPROACHES EMPHASIZING FULFILLMENT AND ACTUALIZATION

Hadley Cantril, another American social psychologist, believed that all personal experiences have a "value quality" and that every person seeks increments in the value quality of experience (Cantril, 1952). Each person has his or her own standard for judging the quality of a new experience, this standard emerging from previous expectations and their subsequent fulfillments. The anticipation of fulfillment is always ambivalent and often poignant, edged on one side by hopes for a better experience than before and on the other by fears that the new experience may actually be worse than the previous one. Thus, we cannot establish a universal standard for fulfillment of the value quality of experience for all humans. Each person must judge fulfillment on the basis of individual norms, expectations, and history, that is, on the basis of his or her own personal standard.

Cantril studied the pattern of concerns of persons living in nations in various levels of development (Cantril, 1965). His analysis suggested that, as nations' levels of development change, so do the nature of the hopes and fears that provide the basis for the value quality in the lives of the citizens of those nations. At the lowest level of national development, people's aspirations do not rise above acquiescence to circumstances; but as levels of development increase, aspirations awaken to an awareness of new potentialities. With higher levels of development comes a recognition of means to attain intended goals, an experiencing of intended consequences through action, and finally a general satisfaction with an attained way of life that promises continued fulfillment. The value quality of an experience to a particular individual at a specific time will depend upon the meaning given that experience by the level of development of the nation and the level of development of that person in that national setting. What one person might experience as greatly satisfying, another might well experience as deprivation.

To study the value quality of experiencing (without being forced to refer to group norms), Kilpatrick and Cantril (1960) developed the Self-Anchoring Striving Scale. The respondents are asked to think of their hopes and fears for themselves and for their nation and are then presented with a ten-rung ladder, being requested to think of the top rung as the best possible world and the bottom rung as the worst possible world. Using these two personal "anchors," the persons are then asked to indicate at which rung they feel they are now, where they were five years ago, and where they feel they will be five years from the time of the rating. Fulfillment is thus understood as occurring in a time frame.

Viktor Frankl, a Viennese psychiatrist, developed the theory that man's primary motivating force is not the will to pleasure nor the will to power but *the will to meaning* (Frankl, 1962, 1965). The meaning of life cannot be known to humans in any proven way, but each person is responsible for finding the meaning of his or her own life, and this meaning of the individual life is found through the search for values. According to Frankl, one may fulfill values by doing a deed (creative values), by experiencing the value quality of another person (experiential values), or by assuming an attitude toward a situation that cannot be changed (attitudinal values). One thus may fulfill values through work, through love, and through suffering. Frankl developed his theory before being confined to the Nazi concentration camp at Auschwitz, and his writings reveal how he found his suffering to be a path to meaning, to personal fulfillment. He was fulfilled as a human being through the attitude he took toward this impossible situation, over which he had no control.

The absence of values is *existential vacuum*, a state of boredom in which nothing matters because nothing has meaning. When anguish comes from the absence of meaning and a desire for it, this is the experience of *existential frustration*. Frankl believed that existential vacuum and frustration are dilemmas and, in fact, tragedies of our modern technological times, and he proposed, as a solution, logotherapy, a values-oriented counseling through which the person is redirected toward a search for, selection of, and fulfillment of values. The anguish of existential frustration can lead, through logotherapy, to a choice of values that will then provide life with a meaning.

Crumbaugh and Maholik (1964) developed the Purpose-in-Life Test to measure the extent of existential vacuum. This test is a fairly short and simple self-rating procedure for obtaining a general estimate of the level of meaningfulness in living experienced by an individual.

Abraham Maslow, noted for his influence in helping to establish a humanistic orientation in American psychology, believed that human values derive from the human's biological nature (Maslow, 1968, 1971). One fulfills oneself through actualizing one's potential as an organism. Capacities become needs, which in turn become the values. When these values are expressed to their fullest, a *peak-experience* results. The peak-experience is a moment of complete fulfillment, a totally engrossing experience that can only be described in terms of B-values ("Being-values"). B-values are all metaphorical and include truth, goodness, beauty, aliveness, simplicity, playfulness, justice, self-sufficiency, etc. Each B-value is a mark of fulfillment yet is but one aspect of a unified, integrated total experience, such as is exemplified by the words used by many women to describe their experience of giving birth to a child when the father is present (Tanzer, 1968).

The Personal Orientation Inventory was developed by Shostrom (1966) to assess the self-actualization of an individual, as defined by Maslow. It consists of a series of paired comparison statements, the choices between which produce a series of scores on Maslowian scales, for example, "Self-actualizing Value" and "Synergy." The P.O.I. was created for use by professional counselors as a tool for evaluating current status and progress through therapy, when such progress is defined as self-actualization.

Maslow also proposed another idea which merges with our next concern, that of valuing competence. He proposed that there are good values and poor values and that the way to identify good values is to study the choices of the good valuers. A good valuer is one who clearly actualizes his or her own potentialities, whose choices satisfy that person's needs as a human organism. The self-actualized person thus becomes the competent valuer, such a valuer being described by Maslow as revealing a more accurate perception of reality, more openness to experience, more unity and integration in the sense of self, and a greater ability to transcend personal limitations than a less self-actualized valuer reveals. To Maslow, self-actualization—fulfillment—and competence are but two aspects of the same phenomenon.

APPROACHES EMPHASIZING COMPETENCE

Robert Hartman, a philosopher who lectured in the United States and in Mexico and whose theories impressed Maslow, attempted to establish a scientific basis for axiology (Hartman, 1967). He proposed that the central question for such a science is, How can you tell when a thing is good? or, stated slightly differently, What is the nature of good-ness? Hartman rather whimsically described his intellectual predecessor, G. E. Moore, as believing that "Good is Good and that is that!" because "What Good-ness is, goodness only knows." Then Hartman proposed the fundamental axiom of scientific axiology: *A thing is good when it fulfills the definition of its concept.* Thus, in order to know the "good-ness" of any "thing," one must know the terms of the definition by which it is being judged.

Concepts differ in the number of terms or components in their definitions; in order to satisfy definition A, three conditions must be met; whereas to satisfy definition B six conditions must be met. According to Hartman, the greater the number of terms an instance is called upon to satisfy, the greater the value of that instance; the fulfillment of a ten-component concept produces greater value than the fulfillment of a two-component concept. Hartman proposed that there are three different kinds of concepts, the fulfillments of which result in three levels of value. Singular concepts refer to unique identities, such as a person, and the fulfillment of a singular concept produces *intrinsic value*; abstract concepts refer to natural properties, such as characteristics of objects, and the fulfillment of this type of concept produces *extrinsic value*; formal concepts refer to ideas, such as a geometric circle, the fulfillment of which produces *systemic value*. Singular-concept definitions comprise more components than abstract-concept definitions, which in turn comprise more components than formal-concept definitions. Therefore, the singular concept can be fulfilled in more ways than can the abstract concept, and the same holds true for abstract over formal. As a result, intrinsic value is greater than extrinsic value, which is greater than systemic value. Concepts, of course, may be combined. Hartman gives the example of adding whipped cream to chocolate pudding as a type of combination which increases the number of ways in which the pudding can fulfill the definition of a dessert, while combining sawdust with the pudding would decrease its potential to fulfill the definition. The various types of combinations that increase or decrease value led Hartman to create what he referred to as "the calculus of formal axiology," the technical procedure by which the value of an instance can be determined exactly through an analysis of the types of concepts, and their combinations, which are applied to that instance.

Hartman emphasized that before we attempt to assess whether a person values beauty over money, we must first determine the person's competency to make such a judgment. This is done through the administration of the Hartman Value Profile (Hartman, 1973). Using the calculus of scientific axiology, Hartman listed eighteen concepts and arranged them from greatest to least number of components, which by definition meant also arranging them from greatest worth to least worth. The person responding to the Hartman Value Profile is asked to rank-order the eighteen concepts according to their worth. These ranks are then compared with the theoretically correct rankings, thereby producing the respondent's score of valuing competence. This competence score thus reflects the degree to which an individual recognizes the extensiveness of the components in a definition, i.e., the number of components that each of a series of instances must satisfy in order to be considered "Good."

John Dewey, a psychologically oriented American philosopher and educator, defined valuation as the process of going from a less satisfactory state of affairs to a more satisfactory state (Dewey, 1939).

Valuing involves an actual unsatisfactory situation, a presumed more satisfactory situation, and the means for going from the unsatisfactory to the anticipated better situation. The importance to an individual of a given state of affairs can be judged only through the attention given to the means for achieving that state of affairs. That is, "prizing," and "caring for" as criteria for a valued state of affairs can be judged only in terms of what a person *does* to bring about the desired conditions, not on the basis of what is *said* to be prized or cared for. Valuing is thus an action-oriented, problem-solving process.

Dewey's influence upon contemporary thinking about valuing most clearly appears in the writings of a group of educators who are attempting to promote the use of the Values Clarification process (Raths, Harmin, and Simon, 1966). Values Clarification is a process for increasing the valuing maturity of individuals through clarifying their relationship to their society. This process is based on the assumption that nothing is a value unless it meets seven criteria: it must be (1) freely chosen (2) from among alternatives (3) after careful consideration; it must then be (4) prized and cherished, (5) publicly affirmed in some form, and (6) acted upon (7) repeatedly. For something to be a value, all criteria must be met; hence, if some, but not all, criteria are met, one has only a "value indicator."

The above criteria determine the nature of values education, the goal of which is to produce effective, competent valuers through an examination of choices and choosing. Competent valuers are seen as persons who select values only after a careful, thoughtful consideration of alternatives, who truly prize and cherish what is valued and willingly affirm these values publicly, and who repeatedly act upon their values.

Because the emphasis of the Values Clarification approach is upon the valuing process, little attention is paid to assessment. The best procedure for assessing valuing competency, as defined by the above criteria, would seem to be the Values Grid (Simon, 1972). An individual is asked to identify the issues that are most important in influencing the quality of his or her life whether a position has been taken on that issue, and whether any such decision was made after careful consideration, publicly affirmed, etc. This procedure is set up in checklist format, allowing for quantitative assessment, though its primary function is as a tool for clarifying the valuing tendencies of the individual. The goal of assessment is not a score but the diagnosis of aspects of valuing that are only weakly developed. With the identification of underdeveloped aspects of valuing, the individual can be guided toward an increasing competence in valuing.

Lawrence Kohlberg, a developmental social psychologist writing in America, suggests that values education should consist of the stimulation of moral development through the encouragement of a capacity for principled moral judgment and a disposition to act in accordance with this capacity (Kohlberg, 1958, 1969, 1971a, 1971b, 1973). Basic hierarchies of moral values are primarily reflections of developmental stages in moral thought. Because moral conflicts are conflicts between competing claims of persons, the basic moral valuing principle is justice. The fundamental forms of justice are equality, or *distributive justice* ("Everyone deserves a decent minimum income") and reciprocity, or *commutative justice* ("Only those who work hard should get the rewards of hard work"). The basis for most arguments about what is just is a dispute over the relative merits of the two forms of justice.

Kohlberg proposed in 1958 that individuals may be classified according to six levels of moral development. At the two lowest levels, moral thinking is based on hedonic consequences; at the next two levels, morality involves normative concern; and at the highest two levels, the individual is guided by principles of justice. Moral development is a cognitive process involving reasoning, and so it can be developed through properly designed exercises. Therefore, values education should be designed to lead a person to higher, and more principled, thinking about moral issues.

Kohlberg used an interview to assess principled moral judgment: he challenged the thinking of respondents by presenting hypothetical situations involving moral dilemmas. A more structured and psychometrically sophisticated instrument for assessment is the Defining Issues Test (Rest, 1974). In this test a hypothetical situation involving a moral dilemma is again used, but the respondent is then presented with a list of issues of varying degrees of relevance to the dilemma. The task for the respondent is to indicate the degree of importance each issue has for the resolution of the dilemma and then to select the four most important issues in the entire list. The P score, or principled moral judgment score, reflects the individual's capacity to determine the central issues for working out a moral dilemma. This score is a single index of the level of principled thinking about moral conflicts, and, as such, it indicates the competence of the individual to make value judgments.

SUMMARY

Axiology, as a branch of ethics, concerns itself with life's values, the nature of the good life, in contrast with deontology, which is concerned with right conduct. Axiology, as a new discipline, still has to define its basic themes of concern. At present there are no truly comprehensive approaches to valuing, only those that focus on one or two facets of valuing.

Five major models for the structure of value system content have been presented: (1) Spranger's six valuing attitudes (economic, theoretic, aesthetic, political, social, religious); (2) Morris's seven Ways to Live (Appollonian, Buddhistic, Christian, Dionysian, Maitreyan, Mohammedan, Promethian); (3) Kluckhohn and Strodtbeck's Value Orientations (nature of man, man-nature relationship, activity, focus in time, man's relationship to man); (4) Rokeach's terminal (personal, social) and instrumental (moral, competence) distinction; and (5) Eckhardt's appeal for a more compassionate world through an emphasis upon freedom *and* equality.

The three models of the nature of valuing fulfillment that were presented included (1) Cantril's analysis of the value quality in experience; (2) Frankl's proposal of the Will-to-Meaning; and (3) Maslow's description of the actualization of human potential.

Four approaches to valuing competency were noted. The three primary models were (1) Hartman's scientific axiology; (2) the Values Clarification modernization of Dewey's theory; (3) Kohlberg's model of principled moral judgment. In addition, Maslow's consideration of self-actualization as a form of valuing competence was noted.

The above approaches represent the range and levels of concerns about values among modern scholars that have resulted in procedures for assessing the valuing of individuals.

3.

The Content and
Organization of Value Systems

CONTEMPORARY RESEARCH on the organization of value systems has generally proceeded along a reductionistic path. To create some order out of the multiplicity of values that people claim to cherish, and to determine whether some groups of valuers are more like each other than they are like all other people, social scientists have turned to the statistical procedures of factor analysis. Through the use of high-speed computers, the responses of people to a large number of statements in a values inventory can be correlated. These correlations may then be factor-analyzed to identify either (1) the minimum number of underlying variables, or *factors*, necessary to account for the major portion of the correlations or (2) the minimum number of groups of persons who share a common value pattern (*types*) that is necessary to account for the major portion of the correlations. In this way the bewildering array of values we believe people hold can be reduced to a shorter list or to a smaller number of value patterns, and, hence, the conceptual structure of the value realm becomes greatly simplified. The reduction of the number of values or value patterns believed to form the basis for the construction of value systems is appealing to scientists because they believe "the simplest explanation is the best one." Such is the principle of parsimony.

To create a value inventory in the first place, one may theorize that the structure of an individual's value system is constructed out of six "basic" values, as in the Allport-Vernon-Lindzey Study of Values (1960), from thirteen value "patterns," as in the Ways to Live Document (Morris, 1956), etc. Such inventories have a theoretical structure, the accuracy of which can be tested scientifically by factor analysis; when one factor-analyzes the correlations between responses to items, does one find the proposed six or thirteen factors?

An alternative way to create a value inventory is to ask people what they value, accumulate those statements, and then factor-analyze the responses. The resulting factor structure is an empirical, inductively determined discovery, and the need for a theory is rather neatly circumvented. An example of such an approach is a study conducted by Gorlow and Noll (1967). These researchers asked seventy-five volunteers from a general psychology class to generate value statements. Some were asked to list "sources of meaning in life," while others were asked to list "goals in life" or "sources of pleasure in life." The resulting fifteen hundred statements were reviewed for overlapping content by a different group of students, who reduced the list to seventy-five "non-overlapping, clearly stated values," each of which was then cast into infinitive form, for example, "to be loved," "to direct others," and so on. These final seventy-five statements were then administered to a wide variety of people ranging in age from sixteen to fifty-four and representing "a large enough variety to allow for the possibility of discovering different and distinct value orientations." The respondents were asked to use the Q-sort response format, a procedure requiring that all the statements be sorted along a continuum from lowest value to highest value, with most of the statements being placed in the very middle and only a few as highest or lowest.

The use of the Q-sort carries with it the assumption that the resulting value systems are organized as relative priority systems rather than as systems containing individually valid, autonomous, absolute principles. The respondent does not rate a value for its own importance, but only for its importance relative to other values. This procedure forces a total set of values into a rank-ordered system and presupposes that most values are of medium importance.

The Q-sorts produced by individuals were then intercorrelated by

Gorlow and Noll, and the resulting matrix of intercorrelations was factor-analyzed. Eight factors (accounting for 65 percent of the total variance) were identified and were labeled *typologies*; that is, in this study the reductionistic approach was used to decrease the number of patterns of response among valuers rather than to decrease the number of variables. Each of the groups of persons identified through the use of the factor analysis was given a label that seemed to characterize the specific value statements emphasized or de-emphasized by the members of the factored type. These patterns of response, or types of valuers, if you will, were (1) *affiliative-romantics* – the values emphasized were reciprocal love, sensitivity to others, and warm emotional responsiveness, while managing, directing, and excelling were de-emphasized; (2) *status-security seekers* – emphasis was given to wealth and status, security, achievement, and sexual prowess, while moral, ethical, and religious values were de-emphasized; (3) *intellectual humanists* – emphasis was given to truth seeking, affiliation with humanitarian efforts, contribution to society, and solidarity with mankind, while success and self-indulgence were de-emphasized; (4) *family valuers* – love, marriage, and children were emphasized in contrast to management, success, and status; (5) *rugged individualists* – solitude, individuality, and independence were the values emphasized, while humanitarian efforts, interest in other persons, loyalty to others, and sharing were de-emphasized; (6) *undemanding passives* – emphasis was placed on general stability and relaxation, with a de-emphasis placed upon striving; (7) *"boy scouts"* – usefulness, optimism, and activity were emphasized, while political wisdom, sex, and physical attractiveness were de-emphasized; (8) *"Don Juans"* – emphasis was given to physical attractiveness, sensuality, and sex, while such family matters as being married, having children, and being on affectionate terms with one's family were de-emphasized.

These findings illustrate two points rather nicely. First, a large number of individuals have been neatly placed in a set of categories. The apparent complexity of individuality among valuers has become simplified through a reduction process. Second, once a category has been identified statistically, its essence has to be reasoned out and captured through a label created to describe the values emphasized by the persons in the category. However titillating such labels as "Don Juan" and "Boy Scout" may be, one should feel free to wonder whether the complex value pattern of a whole group of persons is adequately summarized by such succinct titles. The reader is well advised to remember that he or she has as much right to provide labels for statistically identified factors as the researcher who did the initial labeling.

The Gorlow and Noll study typifies the inductive approach to an analysis of the content and structure of value systems. An item pool of values is established, the responses to the item pool are subjected to a statistical procedure designed to reduce the item pool to a few simplified categories, and the categories are identified with a label that describes the essence of the category in the eyes of the labeler. The generality of this approach is limited by (1) the content of the item pool: the factors determined will be based upon the values that happen to be included in the pool; (2) the nature of the responding group: the factors identified may describe only the membership of a particular subject pool; and (3) the labeling skill of the researcher: the creativity of the labeler may elucidate or confound an understanding of the categories uncovered. We turn now to a review of research based upon theoretical models of the content and organization of value systems.

SPRANGER'S SIX TYPES OF VALUING ATTITUDES

The book that propelled the study of human valuing into the realm of social science was published by Eduard Spranger during the 1920s. His *Types of Men: The Psychology and Ethics of Personality* provided an analysis of valuing that stimulated the design and construction by Philip Vernon and Gordon Allport of the first "test" of values, the Study of Values in 1931 (Vernon and Allport, 1931). Most research on the psychological nature of values during the next thirty years relied upon the use of this instrument, even though the theoretical significance of Spranger's ideas was unfortunately little pursued.

The impetus for Spranger's theory was what he considered to be a most unfortunate trend, the inclination to classify persons according to race, nationality, and genealogy. Such social classifications not only provide the foundation for racial, national, and class differences but also ignore the psychological differences that exist among individuals of the same race, nation, class, or family. What was needed for a further and more correct understanding of the functioning of, and the differences among, humans was a psychological classification system, a way of thinking about persons at a psychological level. The central construct he proposed for such a psychological understanding was *the valuing attitude.*

Each person faces a complex array of life situations that, in themselves, may seem like a series of singular, unrelated events. The sense of integrity, the sense of personal unity in the face of such disjointed events, is found in each person's *dominant value-direction.* The dominant value-direction is determined by the organization of the person's valuing attitudes.

A minor digression is appropriate here. Spranger points out that the term *value* has three interpretations: (1) value *essence*, or the general species of value such as economic value or political value or religious value; (2) the realization of the value essence in an object, such as in a painting where the value essence of beauty is realized; and (3) the realization of a value essence in a personal experience, such as the experience of being in love. This last interpretation of the term is closest to what Spranger refers to as the value-direction of the individual, though he was also concerned with how value essences become translated into value-directions.

Six basic valuing attitudes were proposed by Spranger to be the psychological expressions of the primary valuing essences. Through the ordering of these six valuing attitudes, personally integrating value directions are constructed. Four of these valuing attitudes, the economic, aesthetic, theoretical, and religious, derive from the levels of self identified by Spranger; whereas two others, the social and political, derive from the necessary structure of community life.

Before these are described individually, mention should be made of Spranger's analogy of the prism. Though we perceive light as white, we can through the use of the prism break it up into its component rainbow of colors. With special prisms we can even control the extent to which certain colors predominate over the others. So it is with the valuing of the individual who experiences each moment in life as unitary and singular, i.e., as "white light." Experience can be analyzed into its component and dominant valuing attitudes for the purpose of scientific research; i.e., value analysis is analogous to the use of a prism. But Spranger never lost sight of the fact that such scientific analysis is artificial. The individual experiences the "whiteness" of the actual life situation, as it were, even though as scientists we can break down the whiteness into color bands of varying widths to determine which is most dominant.

The economic valuing attitude, according to Spranger, centers on considerations of utility, on usefulness for the maintenance and preservation of life, and on the fulfillment of needs. Everything is viewed as an aid to the natural struggle for existence and as a possibility for rendering life more pleasant. Goods and forces, time and space, are economized in order to gain the maximum of useful effect. The person whose dominant value-direction is economic strives to free himself or herself from immediate wants. Hence, suggests Spranger, the longing for freedom of action is fundamentally a desire to be free of any wants and therefore qualifies as an economic impulse.

The theoretic valuing attitude is revealed in the impulse toward assigning reasons and developing laws that follow one from another with strict logic and result in the creation of a system. Spranger says:

> Whenever this attitude aiming at objectivity, the attitude which identifies and differentiates, generalizes and individualizes, conjoins and separates, reasons and systematizes, whenever this attitude becomes dominant, it is self-evident that all subjective relations such as feeling and desiring, attraction and repulsion, fearing and hoping, must sink into the background.

The person whose dominant value-direction is theoretic is epitomized as having "only one passion, that for objective knowledge; only one kind of longing, to solve a problem, explain a question or formulate a theory." The theoretic person "does not wish to be an inconsistent entity in a world of order"; hence a longing for inner consistency is a theoretic impulse.

The aesthetic valuing attitude is revealed in two primary characteristics: the will to form and a concentration upon concrete perceptual experience. This valuing attitude is not governed by a concern for utility nor by a concern for general laws of reality but by a desire to create a self in harmony with aesthetic guidelines that generally spring from inner life. The classic aesthetic person is a "virtuoso of life" who makes out of himself a "work of art," the person becoming the epitome of form, beauty, harmony, and proportion. This desire to develop one's imagined self in tangible and perceptual ways reveals that "self-realization, self-fulfillment, self-enjoyment are aesthetic aims . . . a striving for development as a conscious means of shaping one's inner self." Spranger believed that "the final gospel of Ibsen and Wilde" was to "be yourself." The more moderate are guided by a sense of good taste, a sense of tact, or a sense of decorum, and reject a course of action not because it is dangerous or inconsistent but because it lacks style. The sense of balance and moderation is a reflection of the aesthetic valuing attitude.

Spranger contrasts this aesthetic life-style with the more traditional stereotype of the artist who is "concentrated on a single point and has an insatiable longing wholly to express himself in a masterpiece." The productive artist reveals a variant of the aesthetic valuing attitude, whose concern lies in trying to create a painting or other object of beauty that expresses concretely the form that exists in the imagination of the artist, or the form the artist assumes exists in the imagination of all mankind but until the exposition of the masterpiece was inarticulate. The essence of the aesthetic valuing attitude, however, lies in the longing for the development of a self in harmony with an inner imagined self.

The social valuing attitude, according to Spranger, finds its expression through love, love for others as potential carriers of value. The well-being of the other, the value character of the other, outweighs all other motives. Love, surrender, and sacrifice alone truly enrich this social type. This inclination toward another person for the sake of that person's possibilities reveals that the person whose dominant value-direction is social "does not live immediately through himself but in others." This may be carried to the point where the social valuing person sees his or her value only as it is reflected in other people and "the limits of individuation disappear."

The political valuing attitude, in contrast to the social, finds its expression in self-affirmation and self-assertion. The focus of life is upon that dimension of social relations that has at one pole superiority and at the other pole dependency. The search for power is not to be mistaken for the use of force and constraint, which is its ultimate physical consequence. It is, rather, the need "to imprint one's will to value upon the inner world and the external behavior of another." The constant *motive* of the person whose dominant value-direction is political is that he should be superior to everyone else, should maintain advantage and stay at the top at all costs. The art of creating and utilizing opportunities involves use of the self; hence the hallmark of the political valuing attitude is self-control. The self is controlled as a tool for the control of others. Spranger points out that, with the dominance of political valuing, truth becomes "a subordinate and technical tool" for maintaining superiority, that the purpose of rhetoric becomes simply to cajole rather than to convince, and finally that "anyone who is always fighting will soon come to feel that what he wills and believes is a sort of 'self-evident' truth and [will come to] lose all understanding of an objective justly evaluating attitude."

The religious valuing attitude is revealed whenever there is an effort to relate a specific event to the total meaning of life. The search for the value meaning in the world was to Spranger a "religious" effort; and the specific solutions, the religions of mankind, were but the answers of specific men. The essence of the religious valuing attitude is not to be found in the specific solutions but in the seeking of the highest value. Salvation is the experience of the person who "finds the highest value in himself and rests in that," while the person who vacillates as to the highest value "is homeless, torn, despairing." Spranger notes that people who have once felt what they call "grace, the suffusion of their entire being with the highest value," strive again and again for the same experience. The person whose dominant value-direction is religious strives to sense the meaning and highest value in life and, as this is found in personal experience, the highest value differs with each individual.

Hence, the dominantly religious person, though interested in the solutions of others, is not threatened by them.

Each of the valuing attitudes carries with it its own ethics and its own theory of development. Let us first consider the ethical orientations associated with each of the valuing attitudes. The economic valuing attitude has its own utilitarian system of ethics. Because everything is seen as fundamentally subserving the maintenance of life and adaptation to environmental conditions, the system of morals and ethics "not only condones but demands the striving for one's own good." Thus, within an economically oriented society suicide would be unthinkable.

Spranger proposes that the ethics of the theoretic valuing attitude are not the ethics of truth but the ethics of "general legality." The essence of such general legality is the formation of behavior into a closed system and the achievement of consistency of personality. Thus objectivity and lawful order are elevated to ethical status, and to be moral is to live "by maxims," while the ethics of truth are recognized to fall within the province of the social valuing attitude.

The aesthetic valuing attitude is bound by the ethics of inner form, the striving for inner wealth of experience and harmony, the balance between "reason and sensuality," the ethics of good taste.

In contrast, the ethics of the social valuing attitude are found in helpful love and in loyalty and neighborliness. Trust finds its cement in the ethics of truth. The "categorical imperative" of social valuing attitude is to live for the other person. The ethics of the political valuing attitude are those of self-affirmation, self-appreciation, and self-control. According to Spranger, the will to power is a genuine form of ethics, since all power begins with inner self-control.

The ethics associated with the religious valuing attitude come in two forms: (1) the ethics of the highest expansion of life, in which there is an obligation to find meaning through the celebration of all the positive values in life, and (2) the ethics of the greatest limitation of life, in which the specifically religious obligation is the renunciation of the world and the depreciation of the self.

Individuals who become aware of their own personal development are almost certain to judge it according to the style of their own fundamental value-direction. Thus Spranger describes the person whose dominant valuing attitude is theoretic as being inclined to "reduce the process of his development to rational, consciously apprehended steps. He believes . . . that all he has become has been the result of will and choice based on general rules of life." The person who stresses economic values "regards his development as a consequence of purposive adaptations in which each time he has mastered a new phase in life." All activity is viewed as a kind of skilled technique when seen from the economic vantage point.

The person whose dominant value direction is aesthetic tends to believe "that his life was organic. He has assimilated the impressions of life as material, searched for and made a part of his soul new life conditions and thus become what he is: an organic form endowed with soul." If the social valuing attitude predominates, development is reduced to the effects of creative love and nurture, to the profound influence of giving and receiving; whereas persons whose dominant value direction is political consider themselves self-made, through a "deed of freedom." Such persons have conquered the resistance of the dull world by energy of will and created their own sphere of existence; they interpret their character as the result of freely willed deeds.

Religious persons, finally, feel in their development either the grace of God, which has tenderly guided all their steps, or the world-conquering power of their own soul, which has fought for the Divine. Both may be conceived as either a quiet, continuous activity or a sudden conversion or series of conversions in which the highest meaning is revealed.

Spranger tried to establish an objective hierarchy of values. He ranked economic values the lowest and religious the highest. Aesthetic values had equal standing with theoretic, and social values enjoyed equal footing with political. Even so, Spranger made it quite clear that he believed each individual lives according to his or her own value-direction. The value system of the person is an individualized ordering of the six valuing attitudes, embedded in an individualized life context—though, of course, one valuing attitude may become so intense as to become a cardinal value.

Value-directions provide a basis for the individual to relate to unique life circumstances; a value-direction provides organized guidelines that help a person adapt to historically unique situations and events. Hence the model of valuing attitudes is just that: a model. The reality to Spranger was the unique person relating to unique events.

This value system, then, has the effect of (1) organizing the person's perceptions of life events—the person tends to be sensitive to those stimuli that have significance to the value system; and (2) guiding the actions of the person—i.e., the person will seek out those situations that allow for the expression of the value system.

To assess these six valuing tendencies proposed by Spranger, Vernon and Allport (1931) created the Study of Values. Including its revisions (Allport, Vernon and Lindzey, 1960), the Study of Values probably qualifies as the second-oldest psychological inventory in continuous and regular use (the Stanford-Binet test of intelligence is about fifteen years older). A respondent is asked such questions as whether the accomplishment of practical goals or the encouragement of interest in the rights of others is the more important function of modern leaders, whether more time should be spent reading newspaper articles on the stock market or on the latest artistic exposition, and whether the policies of local schools should emphasize music and fine arts, social problems, or laboratory experiences. The responses to forty-five such items are scored to produce a Profile of Values, which measures the preference an individual shows for items reflecting aesthetic, economic, political, religious, social, or theoretic values and reveals in graphic form how the person's scores compare with norms based on scores of some eight thousand American university students. (If desired, secondary school norms are also available.)

Several attempts have been made to check on the validity of Spranger's typology by using factor analysis to assess the relationship of the six types of items to each other. Lurie (1937) did not like the response format and items of the Study of Values; so he revised them. He reported that his factor analysis of an item pool based on the revision of the Study of Values resulted in (1) little evidence for a separate aesthetic scale and (2) little evidence to maintain a separation of the economic and political scales from each other. Thus, he concluded that Spranger's six valuing attitudes could be reduced (on the basis of empirical evidence) to four dimensions: the theoretical, the social, the religious, and the political-economic. Brogden (1952) also designed his own variation of the Study of Values format and items. Its results, when factor-analyzed, resulted in ten meaningful (i.e., interpretable) first-order factors: (1) general aesthetic interest, (2) interest in the fine arts, (3) belief in "culture," (4) antireligious evaluative attitude, (5) antiaggression, (6) humanitarian tendency, (7) interest in science, (8) tendency toward liberalism, (9) theoretic interest, and (10) rugged individualism.

The Lurie and Brogden studies, rather than throwing light on the accuracy of Spranger's model, place us in an even greater quandary. The two studies involved (1) separate revisions of the Study of Values format, which were (2) administered to different subjects some fifteen years apart, the responses of whom were (3) subjected to different formulas for computing factors. Because there are so many possible determinants, it is not clear why one study produced four factors and the other ten. We cannot tell which of the results are simply the result of methodological procedures and which reflect the "true" structure of valuing organization.

A further study by Gordon (1972) produced results reminiscent of the Lurie study conducted some thirty-five years earlier. Gordon took an approach similar to that of the Gorlow and Noll study cited at the beginning of this chapter. He correlated the scores on the Allport-Vernon-Lindzey Study of Values produced by some sixty identifiable groups and then factor-analyzed the matrix of intercorrelations among groups. He reported finding four factors. The first factor was bipolar; groups with positive loading on this factor were labeled *economic-political,* and groups with negative loading were termed *social man.* Male undergraduate business administration students typically earned the former label, while female social work students tended to fall into the latter category. The second factor was labeled *Christian conservative,* a group exemplified by scoutmasters. The third factor was labeled *theoretical* and the fourth, *aesthetic.*

Gordon considered his results to be very similar to Lurie's in that (1) both identified four factors and (2) both believed the Study of Values religious items measured conformity to Christian church practices rather than the search for meaning in each event in life, as proposed by Spranger. The merging of the economic and the political valuing attitudes, and the separateness of the religious and the theoretic valuing attitudes, do seem common results. Lurie, however, found a separate social factor which in Gordon's findings existed only as a polar opposition to the economic-political nexus. In addition, Gordon found evidence for a separate aesthetic factor, which had disappeared in Lurie's analysis.

Though the number of dimensions of valuing identified depends in part on the research procedures used, several general conclusions about Spranger's proposed typology still seem warranted. In general, the empirical analysis of the Sprangerian theoretical model suggests that the search for power and the search for financial security and wealth may be quite intermingled, while the search for truth and order and the satisfaction of following Christian practices seem fairly independent. The separateness of value orientations centered in the expression of love or the search for beauty seems less firmly supported by research findings.

MORRIS'S SEVEN PATHS OF LIFE

Whereas Spranger based his analysis of valuing upon hypothesized levels of self, Charles Morris, an American semanticist and philosopher, was concerned with the great religious and philosophical movements that have influenced and organized the lives of humans. His basic premise was that we seek an orientation that will give us a sense of competence in struggling with an environment that seems ever vaster and more powerful. Through his examination of the great religious and philosophical systems—Buddhism, Christianity, Islam, Taoism, and so on—Morris concluded that each was based on a rank-order preference among three ways in which humans can satisfy their needs in relation to their environment. We can (1) indulge our needs in the immediacy of available resources, (2) reduce our frustrations by doing away with or minimizing our needs, or (3) remake the environment so that it will more adequately serve our needs. There are seven ways to combine these three patterns—releasing, controlling, and remaking—in rank order; they create the basis for seven "Paths of Life." According to Morris, each path produces an orientation that provides humans with a sense of competence in the face of a potentially overpowering world. These paths are the Dionysian ("to experience festivity and solitude in alternation"), the Buddhist ("to cultivate independence of persons and things"), the Promethian ("to constantly master changing conditions"), the Apollonian ("to preserve the best that man has attained"), the Christian ("to show sympathetic concern for others"), the Mohammedan ("to act and enjoy life through group participation"), and the Maitreyan ("to integrate action, enjoyment, and contemplation").

Echoing Spranger's recognition that the word *value* has several meanings, Morris distinguished three uses of the term, which are slightly different from those mentioned by Spranger. He called values expressed in actual behavior *operative values*; whereas those expressed in anticipation or foresight about the desirability of an action he called *conceived values*. For example, the actual drug-taking behavior of an addict indicates his operative values; whereas his statement that it is better not to take drugs is an indication of his conceived values. The central distinction between the two is that conceived values involve symbols and operative values are demonstrated by actual behavior. Morris does say that some interaction between operative and conceived values is the common state. Concepts and behavior are necessarily related, yet are not the same thing.

Morris's third use of the term *value* involves what he calls *object values*. These become operative when we place stress upon the properties of an object. That is, value, in this case, seems resident in the qualities of the object itself rather than in the conception or behavior of the valuer. This type of value is also examined in a subfield of economics called values measurement, in which complex formulas are developed to describe the relative worth of objects. For example, a utility function may be drawn to describe the relative worth of so many bananas compared with so many tomatoes.

Despite Morris's work, in most psychological research the term *values* is used in the sense of "conceived values." Hence, the issue of the relationship of values to behavior is always viable and lively.

To conduct research, Morris wrote a descriptive paragraph about each of the Paths of Life. The paragraphs were shown to respondents with the request that they rate each path on a seven-point scale of preference. Thus, rather than reacting to a series of specific items to produce a cumulative score, respondents respond to a description of a total and presumably integrated and comprehensive pattern of living. For example, according to Morris the "Mohammedan Path of Life" is constructed by giving primary rank to the Dionysian component of "tendencies to release and indulge existing desires," secondary rank to the Promethean component of "active tendencies to manipulate and remake the world," and lowest rank to the Buddhistic component of "tendencies to regulate the self by holding in check the desires." He describes this path of life in paragraph form as follows:

> WAY 5: A person should not hold on to himself, withdraw from people, keep aloof and self-centered. Rather merge oneself with a social group, enjoy cooperation and companionship, join with others in reso-lute activity for the realization of common goals. Persons are social and persons are active: life should merge energetic group activity and coop-erative group enjoyment. Meditation, restraint, concern for one's self-sufficiency, abstract intellectuality, solitude, stress on one's possessions all cut the roots which bind persons together. One should live out-wardly with gusto, enjoying the good things of life, working with others to secure the things which make possible a pleasant and energetic social life. Those who oppose this ideal are not to be dealt with too tenderly. Life can't be too fastidious.

The Maitreyan Way, which involves an equal balancing of all three basic components, is described thus:

> WAY 7: We should at various times and in various ways accept something from all other paths of life, but give no one our exclusive allegiance. At one moment one of them is more appropriate; at another moment, another is the most appropriate. Life should contain enjoy-ment and action and contemplation in about equal amounts. When we

carry either to extremes we lose something important for our life. So we must cultivate flexibility, admit diversity in ourselves, accept the tension which this diversity produces, find a place for detachment in the midst of enjoyment and activity. The goal of life is found in the dynamic interaction of the various paths of life. One should use all of them in building a life, and no one alone.

The reactions of some of the persons who were initially asked to respond to these seven paths were very interesting to Morris because the reactions indicated a search for paths not included among the seven listed. So six more paths, or patterns of living, were created based on the comments of these early respondents. Of these six additional paths, three represented other traditional patterns: the Epicurean ("to live with wholesome, carefree enjoyment"), the Taoist ("to wait in quiet receptivity"), and the Stoic ("to control the self stoically"). The final three paths were built inductively from respondents' comments about what concerned them. These paths were: Way 11 – "to meditate on the inner life," Way 12 – "to chance adventuresome deeds," and Way 13 – "to obey the great cosmic purposes." This last path was elaborated as follows:

WAY 13 – A person should let himself be used. Used by other persons in their growth, used by the great objective purposes in the universe which silently and irresistibly achieve their goal. For persons and the world's purposes are dependable at heart, and can be trusted. One should be humble, constant, faithful, uninsistent. Grateful for the affection and protection one needs, but undemanding. Close to persons and to nature, and secure because close. Nourishing the good by devotion and sustained by the good because of devotion. One should be a serene, confident, quiet vessel and instrument of the great dependable powers which move to their fulfillment.

Morris combined these final six ways together with the descriptions of the seven initially theorized paths to create a research inventory he called The Ways to Live Document. This inventory was primarily administered in the twenty years following the middle 1940s to national groups of university students in widely scattered locations.

We can use one very interesting study from this series to illustrate a typical research finding. The Ways to Live Document was administered to a sample of students in mainland China just before the establishment of the current Communist government (Morris, 1956), and comparable data were obtained from a sample of university students in the United States. These data reveal that for the Chinese, sample Way 13 was the highest ranked Way of Life (based on group mean scores) while Way 7 was ranked sixth of thirteen. In contrast, the United States students produced group means that ranked Way 7 highest and Way 13 lowest. Hence, even before the establishment of a new national government in China during the late 1940s, there were striking differences between the values of students in China and in the United States, differences that amount to near-opposite preferences for two central paths of life.

One implication of this finding is that the basic value orientations of the citizens of the two nations seem to have been so drastically different that they led to quite divergent socioeconomic-political ideologies. The media propaganda emanating from the two national groups emphasized for years the competing (negating? rejecting?) implications of the two systems when much greater attention could have been given to harmony within each system between the political organization and the value orientations of the citizens. Apparently, these values orientations were of such great contrast for the valuers that the social systems favored by each were initially, and mutually, perceived as a threat to the other. Attention to the values data in the Morris study could have provided a more balanced perspective on the differences and the harmony between the two world views, as there were shared value priorities as well as the distinctive priorities noted above.

A central question for Morris was whether the structure of value systems was universal; when the responses of, for example, Norwegian students were factor-analyzed, would the same underlying factors be identified as those found in a factor analysis of the responses of students from India? Would the same factors be found even if the profile of values, the priorities, in each group were distinctive? Morris was somewhat noteworthy in that he did not allow his original theory to prevent him from adding six extra Paths of Life to the great historical ones and in that he himself was interested in validating his original theoretical model through factor analysis.

The results of his research were (1) the identification of five value factors, and (2) the verification of similar value structures among student groups from the United States, India, Norway, China, and Canada (in the late 1940s) even though the value profiles, the priorities, of the separate groups were in some cases quite distinct. Morris labeled the factors (1) social restraint and self-control, (2) enjoyment and progress in action, (3) withdrawal and self-sufficiency, (4) receptivity and sympathetic concern, and (5) self-indulgence. As with all factor-analytic results, the names were created from a perusal of the loadings each Way of Life had on each factor plus Morris's personal inclinations about what it all meant.

A somewhat different approach to the analysis of the Ways to Live Document was taken by Gorlow and Barocas (1965), who extracted sixty-three separate statements from the paragraphs of the document. Fifty undergraduate students taking a psychology course were asked to Q-sort the sixty-three statements, and the Q-sort thrown by each person was correlated with the one thrown by everyone else, following which the interperson correlation matrix was factor-analyzed. Six factors were identified, and the meaning of each factor was determined by examining the value statements correlated with it. The individuals identified by the first factor not only emphasized a sympathetic concern for others and a need for affectionate involvement with them, but they also coupled these with a concern for ultimate values. Those high on the second factor emphasized the unselfish use of the self for the growth of others, coupled with a rejection of cultivating an inner self, of isolating and of restraining oneself. The distinctive features of the third factor involved the rejection of an active, energetic life for an emphasis upon inner cultivation and contemplation. A life full of variety and flexibility, full of zest, was associated with the fourth factor; whereas the fifth factor centered on the assertion that the life to lead was one involving energetic action and the excitement of power, with orderliness being clearly rejected. The sixth factor appeared to the researchers to be an active, outward interest in people and living, an "affectional extraversion."

Gorlow and Barocas thus turned away from Morris's search for integrated relationships within complex patterns of living, which he considered unitary expressions of the various arrangements of priorities among the releasing, controlling, and remaking tendencies. Their approach was to divide Morris's patterns into subunits and then to examine the empirical relationships among the subunits. As a result, their research moved away from what may well have been the main merit in Morris's approach, the effort to relate the structure of an individual value system to the great religious and philosophical ideologies which appear to have guided momentous historical movements. Despite such turning away, the results of their research are markedly similar to Morris's own findings. The releasing tendencies hypothesized by Morris found empirical expression in Morris's fifth factor, self-indulgence, and in Gorlow and Barocas's fourth factor, zest and flexibility. Remaking tendencies emerged empirically in Morris's second factor, enjoyment and progress in action, and in Gorlow and Barocas's fifth factor, energetic action and excitement of power. The controlling tendency appears to have found expression in two factors in Morris's data, the first factor, social restraint and self-control, and the third factor, withdrawal and self-sufficiency. The same tendency seems represented in Gorlow and Barocas's third factor, inner cultivation. One factor is left over in Morris's own results, receptivity and sympathetic concern, and three remain in the Gorlow and Barocas results, namely, sympathetic concern, use of the self for the growth of others, and active interest in people. All of these theoretically residual factors are socially oriented, suggesting that even though Morris did not explicitly posit a socializing tendency, such a psychological orientation emerges from the responses of people to his document.

A major weakness in the above type of research is that it is conducted with developing individuals, students whose value systems may not yet have crystallized. None of the studies reported in this chapter were conducted with experienced leaders of the great religio-philosophical systems. Indeed, one might wonder whether such leaders would even be willing to participate as research subjects if informed of the purpose of such research.

ROKEACH'S TERMINAL AND INSTRUMENTAL VALUES

Even during the short life of the Rokeach Value Survey (Rokeach, 1973), it has emerged as the first real challenger to the Allport-Vernon-Lindzey Study of Values as *the* tool for conducting research on human valuing. Milton Rokeach is an American social psychologist who for many years was concerned with the organization of attitude and belief systems (Rokeach, 1960). He finally construed values as the psychological phenomenon most fundamental to an understanding of the individual (Rokeach, 1973). Values, to Rokeach, are prescriptive or proscriptive beliefs, which, because they identify preferable modes of conduct or end states, serve as standards of judgment for the individual. These standards lead us to take stands on social issues, predispose us to favor certain ideologies, guide the way we present ourselves to others, orient the blame and praise we give to people (including ourselves), provide norms for judging morality and competence, influence the ways we try to persuade others, and tell us how to rationalize actions we would ordinarily find unacceptable. Rokeach describes two major types of values: terminal and instrumental. Terminal values are end states, many of which have become institutionalized and are promoted by specific social institutions; for example, wisdom is promoted as a value by educational institutions. Instrumental values are primarily matters of style in behavior, the ways we feel we should go about behaving. There are far more instrumental values than terminal — several dozen of the latter; whereas there may be hundreds of instrumental values.

Rokeach proposed that values are the conceptual tools we use to maintain and enhance self-esteem. He said that all of a person's attitudes can be regarded as value expressive, and that all of a person's values are directed toward maintaining and enhancing "the master sentiment of self-regard." Thus self-esteem is the central psychological motive. Values form the basis for positive self-regard by guiding our adjustment to life situations, by furnishing us with ready-made ways of reducing ego threat, and by providing us with direction in our search for meaning and self-actualization.

He proposed further that the value systems of all persons comprise the same values, the differences among persons being the order of priority given to these values. Value systems are constructed to provide ready-made resolutions of potential conflicts between values. We learn most values on an absolute, all-or-none basis. For example, we are taught "You must never lie!" but as we mature we are faced with conflicts between "You must never lie!" and "You must never hurt the feelings of a friend!" which we also learned on an absolute, all-or-none basis. We are forced to learn that values are relative to each other. To prevent ourselves from being in constant turmoil over choosing courses of action, we prioritize values. Value *systems* are created when one person decides always to tell the truth "no matter how much it hurts," while another decides that people's feelings are always more important than "any little white lie." Hence, a value system consists of the personal hierarchy among the values that are universally included in such systems.

To assess the personal value systems of individuals, Rokeach created the Value Survey, consisting of two sets of eighteen values each—one of instrumental values and the other of terminal values. The respondent to the survey is asked to rank-order the eighteen values in each set. The terminal values to be ranked are presented in the following order: A Comfortable Life (a prosperous life); An Exciting Life (a stimulating, active life); A Sense of Accomplishment (lasting contribution); A World at Peace (free of war and conflict); A World of Beauty (beauty of nature and the arts); Equality (brotherhood, equal opportunity for all); Family Security (taking care of loved ones); Freedom (independence, free choice); Happiness (contentedness); Inner Harmony (freedom from inner conflict); Mature Love (sexual and spiritual intimacy); National Security (protection from attack); Pleasure (an enjoyable, leisurely life); Salvation (saved, eternal life); Self-respect (self-esteem); Social Recognition (respect, admiration); True Friendship (close companionship); Wisdom (a mature understanding of life). The instrumental values to be ranked are Ambitious (hardworking, aspiring); Broad-minded (open-minded); Capable (competent, effective); Cheerful (lighthearted, joyful); Clean (neat, tidy); Courageous (standing up for your beliefs); Forgiving (willing to pardon others); Helpful (working for the welfare of others); Honest (sincere, truthful); Imaginative (daring, creative); Independent (self-reliant); Intellectual (intelligent, reflective); Logical (consistent, rational); Loving (affectionate, tender); Obedient (dutiful, respectful); Polite (courteous, well-mannered); Responsible (dependable, reliable); Self-controlled (restrained, self-disciplined).

Although Rokeach believed the two sets of values "represent two separate yet functionally interconnected systems," he did not delineate in any detail the relationship between the two realms. And although his theory of valuing is as complex and detailed as those of Spranger and Morris, his listing of values seems just that, a list of discrete values that are not organized among themselves in any systematic way.

Two analyses of the internal structure of the Value Survey have been conducted. Rokeach himself factor-analyzed the intercorrelation of the rankings of a representative sample of 1,409 Americans over the age of twenty-one. He identified seven factors which he considered weak because they accounted for only 40 percent of the variance among the rankings. Hence, he concluded there was little empirical support for reducing the number of values in the survey. The seven factors were (1) immediate versus delayed gratification (A Comfortable Life and Pleasure versus Wisdom and Inner Harmony); (2) competence versus religious morality (Logical and Imaginative versus Salvation and Forgiving); (3) self-constriction versus self-expansion (Obedient and Polite versus Broadminded and Capable); (4) social versus personal orientation (A World at Peace and National Security versus True Friendship and Self-respect); (5) societal versus family security (A World of Beauty and Equality versus Family Security and Ambitious); (6) respect versus love (Social Recognition and Self-respect versus Mature Love and Loving); and (7) other-directed versus inner-directed (Polite versus Courageous and Independent).

Feather and Peay (reported in Feather, 1975) conducted a multidimensional scaling procedure with the responses of 548 students at Flinders University in Australia. The procedure, newly created by Peay, is important because the statistical requirements are appropriate to the type of data obtained from the Value Survey, that is, ranked data. The use of factor-analytic procedures is, in fact, based on assumptions that it may not be appropriate to make about Value Survey data.

Using rather stringent criteria for what could be included in the results of the multidimensional scaling procedure, Feather and Peay reported the identification of five major dimensions around which the thirty-six values could be arranged. The first dimension consists of a contrast between (a) Obedient, Responsible, Family Security, and Self-Control and (b) Imaginative, Intellectual, Broad-minded, and An Exciting Life. The researchers considered this to be a distinction between discipline and ability, but other possible labels occur to this author, including conservative versus liberal orientation, or even "straight" versus "mod." The second dimension consists of a contrast between (a) Capable, Ambitious, A Comfortable Life, and An Exciting Life, and (b) Forgiving, Helpful, Loving, and A World of Beauty, which appeared to Feather and Peay to be a contrast between a concern for oneself and a concern for others. The contrast in the third dimension is between (a) Wisdom, A Sense of Accomplishment, Logical, and Self-respect and (b) Cheerful, Happiness, Pleasure, Clean, Family Security, and A Comfortable Life. In one way this contrast appears to represent a distinction between a competence orientation against a pleasance orientation. Yet in another view it could be considered a difference between task orientation and mood orientation. The fourth dimension consists of a contrast between (a) Social Recognition, True Friendship, Mature Love, and Happiness and (b) A World at Peace, Freedom, National Security, and Equality, which appeared to be a personal versus a social orientation. The contrast in the fifth dimension consists of (a) Clean, Polite, A Comfortable Life, Cheerful, and Pleasure, as against (b) Inner Harmony, Courageous, Self-respect, and Self-controlled. The researchers considered this dimension parallel to Rokeach's "immediate versus delayed gratification" factor, although they also believed a case could be made for a distinction between pleasant decorum and inner integrity. The researchers agree with Rokeach generally in that they did not believe understanding would increase through a simplification of the Value Survey.

A comparison of Rokeach's factors with Feather and Peay's dimensions suggests at least a partial overlap between four factors/dimensions. Wisdom and Pleasure provide key contrast values in Rokeach's first factor and in Feather and Peay's third dimension; whereas Obedient and Broad-minded provide key contrast values in Rokeach's third factor and in Feather and Peay's first dimension. True Friendship and National Security provide key contrast values in both the fourth factor and the fourth dimension; whereas in Rokeach's seventh factor and in Feather and Peay's fifth dimension Polite and Courageous provide the key contrast in values. Rokeach's second, fifth, and sixth factors and Feather and Peay's second dimension do not appear to be reflected in a comparative analysis.

The effect of requesting respondents to rank value statements rather than to rate each value independently clearly appears in the different kinds of factors or dimensions identified; i.e., the Rokeach Value Survey factors are all bipolar. Axiology has not progressed as a field to the point where any evidence indicates whether values do operate, in fact, as absolute standards or as relative priorities. Until such evidence is forthcoming, the most "Broad-minded" point of view might be that values may operate for some people at some times as absolute standards and for some people at other times as relative priorities. In the meantime the results of the analysis of the Value Survey provide a relative-priority perspective on the organization of value systems, while the results of the research on the Study of Values and the Ways to Live Document provide an absolute-standard perspective.

In all fairness to Rokeach, it should be emphasized that he was not especially preoccupied with the structure of value systems. He was far more interested in the effects of experimentally making an individual dissatisfied with the relationship between the priority given a value and the way in which that value was expressed in behavior. The Value Survey was primarily a tool that allowed Rokeach to test hypotheses about what changes in values or behavior might result from such dissatisfaction. For example, in a series of studies reported in "Long-range experimental modification of values, attitudes and behavior" (Rokeach, 1971), he exposed experimental subjects to conditions designed to arouse their dissatisfaction with their rankings of Equality in the Value Survey in comparison to their rankings of Freedom, and also to arouse dissatisfaction with the relationship between the priority given to Equality and their behavior (or lack of behavior) on civil rights matters. The experimentally created dissatisfaction resulted in changes in the priorities given to both Equality and Freedom (both increased significantly in rank-order) and also led to changes in behavior (for example, the probability of sending money to or joining the National Association for the Advancement of Colored People).

Rokeach ended this report with three searching questions: "Who shall decide which values are to be changed and who shall decide the direction of such change?" "Is it ethically possible to defend experimental work that may lead to relatively enduring changes in a person's values, attitudes and behavior without his informed consent?" and "To what extent should our educational institutions shape values as well as impart knowledge, and, if so, which values and in which direction?"

Rokeach, in his research and in his recognition of its implications, may well have shown us the borderlines of a potential science of human behavior that would center on the manipulation and control of human experience and action. There may well be human potential for experience and action about which we may never learn because to conduct the pertinent research would be unethical. The boundaries of human knowledge *are* defined by ethical considerations, though one is startled to confront such a boundary while trying to gain knowledge about valuing. In a peculiar yet pertinent way, one's values limit what one can know about valuing.

Before we leave Rokeach, special credit should be given to his thoughtful, incisive, and articulate review of the distinctions that can be made between the term *value* and other words that are often used synonymously, such as *attitude, need, social norm, trait,* or *interest.* One of the most perplexing matters for the student of valuing is the undefined and even contradictory use of terms by scholars who show little concern for the resulting confusion of their readers. At times, students begin to feel they are not studying valuing but only sentences about valuing. Rokeach's carefully considered distinctions among terms should be helpful to the student and, if acknowledged by scholars, could well clarify professional communication about valuing.

TWO OTHER APPROACHES

Chapter 2 mentioned the model of value content and structure proposed by Kluckhohn and Strodtbeck (1961) as well as the attempt by Eckhardt (1972) to promote a unifying value orientation. These two approaches are of special note because of their contribution to an understanding of the role of valuing in social conflict. The Kluckhohn and Strodtbeck model has been applied to an understanding of intergenerational conflict within immigrant families in America by Papajohn and Speigel (1975), but, with one exception (Mezei, 1974), no attempt has been made to further analyze their instrument, possibly because it requires oral administration. It therefore consumes more time than most researchers have available for gathering the amount of data necessary for factor analysis. The Eckhardt model, in contrast, provides an a priori, unidimensional value factor, "Compassion," around which all other values are organized. Hence, the simplification is built into the model.

It should now be clear that the primary research instruments for assessing personal value systems are the Allport-Vernon-Lindzey Study of Values, the Morris Ways to Live Document, and the Rokeach Value Survey. The reduction of Spranger's six valuing attitudes to four, of Morris's thirteen Ways to Live to five, and of Rokeach's thirty-six values to seven, though of academic interest, has led neither to a revision of any of the instruments nor to the creation of a "universal" instrument that combines the results of research on all the previously designed surveys. There seems to be an integrity in each test that derives from its relationship to its own theoretical perspective. On the other hand, the theoretical perspectives appear to have remained relatively uninfluenced by the results of empirical examination.

A CONTRASTING POINT OF VIEW

Two assumptions have been made by all the scholars reviewed to this point — (1) that the value system of every person is constructed out of the same values, and (2) that those universal values have been included in the inventory created by the scholars or their students. An alternative hypothesis is that every person's value system is unique in its content and in its organization. Two value systems may overlap in content and may be very similar in structure, but they are never identical. Such an alternative has been proposed in *Values Exploration* (Simmons, 1978), an approach to valuing developed by the author. To stimulate the thinking of students enrolled in a course on counseling and psychotherapy, the author developed a list of one hundred values by sampling the writings of Spranger, Morris, and Rokeach but also including values proposed by Maslow (Maslow, 1968; Tanzer, 1968), Cantril (1965), and several authors in the July 1967 issue of the *Journal of Social Issues* devoted to "Stirrings out of apathy: Student activism and the decade of protest" (Flacks, 1967; Sampson, 1967). Included as well were the notions of the author at that time about the structure and content of value systems. This set of values was considered a broadband spectrum, as it was not limited to one theoretical perspective yet had its roots in the major theoretical models of personal valuing.

The survey was originally administered as a forced-choice Q-sort: each value was placed on a separate one-by-three-inch card, and the students in the class were instructed to assume that they were the ideal counselor and to sort out the values as if they held that role. The purpose was to disclose the implicit assumptions of the students about the values counselors should hold.

Some students asked if they could do the Q-sort for themselves, later reporting that it was a stimulating and for some an insight-provoking experience. Several students commented, however, that the forced-choice distribution was an artificial requirement that didn't allow them to sort out their values accurately. This complaint led to the creation of a free-sorting procedure in which respondents were first asked to discard from the set of 100 value statements any that they did not consider a value for them and to add any values that were part of their value system but were not included in the original set. Then, with each value statement on a separate card, the respondents were allowed to sort out the values in any way desired and describe the sorting in whatever way seemed appropriate.

The consequence of such free-sorting by respondents was an array of unique value systems. Individual differences occurred in:

1. The number of values included within value systems.

2. The way students sorted out their systems—some used high and medium and low categories along a single dimension, while others used only content categories such as family values and work values and social values.

3. The organization of value patterns—e.g., as a "star" (one central category with several related categories extending from the center), as a "snake" (a pure hierarchy of noncategorized values that had to be "snaked" back and forth on the table in order to fit the available space), as a "circle" (a dozen or so content categories, all of equal importance yet arranged in a circle because each is somewhat more related to its neighbors than to more distant categories), or as a "ski slope" (the values being arranged in order of importance with fewer and fewer values in each category as the students moved toward the least important categories).

4. The presence or absence of negative values in a value system—for example, "These are values I emphatically reject and I believe it important to continue to reject them and to be alert to their insidious influence."

5. The clarity of the system to the observer—a few systems seemed either confused or confusing.

6. The expressions regarding the stability of the value system—for example, "If I do this tomorrow I'll probably do it differently."

7. The expressions of commitment to the system—for example, "Well, that's it, but I don't really feel very strongly about it."

Observation of the free-sorting procedure led to a number of propositions. First, values exist only as components in a uniquely organized value system. Second, each value has a life history of its own. Third, value systems are dynamic, often changing and reorganizing in response to external *and* internal procedures. Fourth, value systems are structured as partial hierarchies. Fifth, the inclusion of certain values in the system will influence the structure of the system; for example, valuing "a sense of everything being connected" will tend to reduce both the number of other values included in the system and the way those that are included relate to each other. These propositions suggest that a scientific goal of simplifying by reducing the number of universal values in a value content inventory can mislead when one wishes to understand the valuing of an individual. Because valuing is a complex, and an individual, process, it should be understood at the level of the individual; the content and organization of an individual value system is unique and changing, not universal and static. The most appropriate way to assess such a value system would be to provide as many values for reaction as possible to the individual in order to determine what is included or excluded from the system, how the values included in the system are organized into categories, and how those categories are related to each other. In addition, in order to understand the growth and development of the system, there is the necessity of repeating the whole process at various time intervals.

The theories of the scholars reviewed are extremely important, for they identify the major types of values that emerge from a consideration of the nature of self, of the great philosophical systems, and of the primary social institutions around which living patterns are organized. The theories have provided us with clues as to the content of value systems, have alerted us to the need for empirical research on the nature and functioning of value systems, and have identified for us a host of problems regarding valuing, for example the issue of absolute value standards versus relative priority systems.

SUMMARY

The variety of apparent values has led scientists to apply the principle of parsimony to the analysis of value systems, primarily through the use of factor analysis to reduce in number the categories of *basic values* presumed to exist and/or the number of different *types of valuers*. The search for the simplest structure of value systems concentrated on results obtained through the three major instruments for assessing the content of a value system, with the number of factors identified varying from study to study. Factor analyses of the Allport-Vernon-Lindzey Study of Values produced a reduction of Spranger's six valuing attitudes to four, namely, political-economic, theoretical, religious, and social (in one study) or aesthetic (in another study). Factor analyses of the Morris Ways to Live Document reduced the thirteen Paths of Life to five factors in one case and six in another. Morris's three human tendencies—releasing, controlling, and remaking—were reflected in both factor analyses but both also identified a social valuing factor that he had not proposed. Morris's own research results suggested that controlling tendencies may in fact be of two kinds: Stoic (social restraint and self-control) and Buddhistic (withdrawal and self-sufficiency). The Rokeach Value Survey, when analyzed, produced seven weak bipolar factors and, when subjected to multidimensional scaling procedures, five bipolar dimensions. Common to both approaches were contrasts illustrated here by four pairs of values: (1) Wisdom versus Pleasure, (2) Obedient versus Broad-minded, (3) True friendship versus National Security, and (4) Polite versus Courageous.

An alternative proposal is presented suggesting that value systems are uniquely organized both as to content and as to structure and in addition are dynamically changing and developing. A procedure whereby the unique value system of an individual may be assessed is described.

4.

The Fulfillment and Actualization of Values

Does one become fulfilled as a valuer when one chooses to commit oneself to certain values, or does fulfillment come only when these values are expressed in action? Is it one's responsibility to find fulfillment in impossible situations, or does fulfillment occur only with the means and opportunity to implement one's inner choices? Is fulfillment a matter of expressing inner potential or of increasing the quality of experience to a higher level than had occurred previously? Such questions as these highlight some of the distinctive concerns of the three theorists who have focused most closely upon the fulfillment and actualization of the values.

Viktor Frankl (1962), Abraham Maslow (1968), and Hadley Cantril (1965) agree that fulfillment of values is a subjective state that reflects environmental conditions yet is not caused directly by them. The individual interprets and gives personal significance to the events that occur around and within him or her. This process of finding significance and, through it, gaining a sense of personal fulfillment has attracted far more theorizing than research. The emergence of research during the 1970s on the subjective quality of life promises to change that situation considerably, especially because the attempt to identify objective social indicators has failed to result in the creation of particularly useful indices of the quality of life. The search for objective indicators seems to be slowly giving ground to the search for more subjective data on the quality of life, such as interested Frankl, Maslow, Cantril, and their students.

THE SEARCH FOR MEANING: FRANKL

Viktor Frankl, a Viennese psychiatrist who developed a psychological theory that challenged those of his older contemporaries Sigmund Freud and Alfred Adler, carried his theory in book form with him to the Nazi concentration camps (Frankl, 1962, 1965). The book was taken from him, and at Auschwitz he was subjected to the gross attempts at dehumanization so effectively portrayed in the media. Frankl, however, did not succumb to these cruelties. He lived through the experience to rewrite his book, in which his theory emphasizes not man's lust for pleasure or power but man's search for meaning. For, as Frankl so clearly states, the primary motive of humans is the *will to meaning*.

Meaning is found through values, of which there are three kinds. We find meaning through what we do (creative values), through our appreciation of sensory experiences and of the inner being of others (experimential values), and through the attitude we take toward those unfortunate circumstances over which we have no control (attitudinal values). Hence, the meaning of life for each of us is not found in abstract generalizations, or in ideology, but through tasks, concrete experiences, and specific attitudes. And each of us is responsible for finding our own fulfillment in living through our personal commitments to these concrete and specific assignments.

The universe, and life, may have an ultimate purpose. The poignancy in human living is that we are unable to prove without a doubt whether there is such a purpose and, if so, just what it is. In such a "not-being-able-to-prove" condition, each of us has the responsibility to choose, and commit to, a meaning in living unique to ourselves, recognizing at the same time that there is no way of knowing whether such a choice will ultimately prove correct.

To refuse to choose because there is no way to prove whether one is right or wrong leads to a psychological state Frankl describes as *existential vacuum*. This state is characterized primarily by boredom, a sense that nothing is more important than anything else. But, because nothing is important, nothing is fulfilling. Fulfillment can come only with goals, with purpose. And humans are free to choose their goals in living. The uniqueness of the human species in nature lies in just this ability to ask, What is the meaning of the universe? and to recognize that, because there is no way of knowing for sure, each human must choose his or her own meaning. Each of us must find some specific, concrete assignment that demands fulfillment. The choice of such an assignment, or goal-for-oneself, produces tension, a tension between oneself and the meaning to be fulfilled. This tension produces mental health and a sense of purpose in life. Hence, we find ourselves with the paradox that what makes life meaningful is the potential that calls for struggle, the lack of fulfillment. When meaning is fulfilled, the assignment accomplished, the struggle over, then the tension is gone and life no longer has meaning—until we choose a further assignment for ourselves. The paradox? Valuing fulfillment is found only through lack of fulfillment! (Frankl does add that potentialities when actualized become realities; they become "What I am in what I have been." But stopping in time is not possible short of death, and so one has to choose another transitory potentiality to find further meaning.)

Values are *pulls*. Humans are not driven or pushed by values. We are free to choose our values, and these choices provide us with a sense of vitality. Yet we do not find these values in ourselves but discover them in the world. To choose to become self-actualizing, according to Frankl, cannot be a goal in itself. Self-actualization comes only as a by-product of our strivings toward values. As we discover values outside of ourselves, the seeking of them leads to self-transcendence, a going beyond ourselves. We find meaning in the nurturing of a friend, in the appreciation of a beautiful landscape, in the attitude taken toward the death of a parent, but not in ourselves. But through such self-transcendence comes self-actualization.

The major research tool derived from Frankl's theory is the Purpose-in-Life Test, designed by Crumbaugh and Maholik (1964) to measure existential vacuum (though scored in such a way that high scores indicate a sense of meaningfulness). Part A of the Purpose-in-Life Test (P-I-L) is scored objectively. The respondent may complete a statement stem such as "I am usually . . ." by circling the number 1 to indicate "completely bored," the number 4 to indicate "neutral," the number 7 to indicate "exuberant, enthusiastic," or if the respondent feels so inclined, any of the intermediate numbers. Part A has 20 statement stems, and the numbers circled by the respondent are added to establish a total score. A theoretically neutral score would be 80 (4 times 20). The lowest possible score, indicative of existential vacuum, is 20; the highest is 140.

Three types of research have been conducted with the Purpose-in-Life Test: (1) the average scores of groups of persons believed to vary in their value fulfillment have been compared; (2) the scores on the Purpose-in-Life Test have been correlated with scores on other indices thought to be related to existential vacuum; and (3) P-I-L scores have been used to assess the effect of logotherapy, the clinical counseling approach derived from Frankl's psychology; tests have been administered before and after such therapy to see whether the client gains an increased sense of fulfillment in living.

In the first line of research, Crumbaugh (1968) found that two groups of persons not subject to psychiatric care averaged 124 and 116 respectively on the Purpose-in-Life Test and that each of two groups of persons under outpatient psychiatric care averaged 101; Crumbaugh and Maholik (1964) found that a group of persons hospitalized for psychiatric care for alcoholism averaged 89. Other findings in this area include an average score of 119 for a group of Dominican Sisters in training (Crumbaugh, Raphael, and Shrader, 1970) and an average score of 96 for a group of persons hospitalized for schizophrenia (Crumbaugh, 1968). Crumbaugh and Maholik have taken these findings to support the validity of the test because its scores discriminate between groups of persons who were expected to differ in the sense of fulfillment they experience in living.

The second line of research consists of exploring the relationship of the fulfillment of the values to other psychological variables by correlating the Purpose-in-Life Test with other selected tests. For instance, statistically significant negative correlations have been found between the Purpose-in-Life Test and Srole's measure of Anomie (Crumbaugh, 1968), the Depression scale of the Minnesota Multiphasic Personality Inventory (Crumbaugh, 1968), the Neuroticism scale of the Eysenck Personality Inventory (Pearson and Sheffield, 1974), and the Anxiety scale on Cattell's 16-PF Test (Crumbaugh, Raphael, and Shrader, 1970). Hence, a low score on the Purpose-in-Life Test, indicating existential vacuum, is significantly associated with a variety of independently developed measures of psychological discomfort and alienation. Boredom, the research seems to suggest, can be psychologically painful. High scores on the Purpose-in-Life Test, on the other hand, were significantly related to high scores on the Self-confidence scale on the Cattell 16-PF Test (Crumbaugh, Raphael, and Shrader, 1970), the Sociability component of the Eysenck Personality Inventory scale for assessing Extraversion (Pearson and Sheffield, 1974), and the Identity Achievement Scale (Simmons, 1980), an indication that the greater the fulfillment of the valuer, the greater the self-confidence, sociability, and sense of personal identity.

The further finding that Purpose-in-Life Test scores were related to proficiency ratings in a training program for Dominican Sisters suggests that a sense of fulfillment may be related to performance adequacy (Crumbaugh, Raphael, and Shrader, 1970). Whether this is a general relationship or a highly specific relationship between commitment to a most distinctive training program and success in that program remains to be seen. There is also no information at this time to determine whether performance adequacy results in a sense of fulfillment, whether feeling a sense of fulfillment increases performance adequacy, or whether the two aspects of living are so intertwined that they flow together without a causative direction being detectable.

The third line of research is highlighted by a report on a logotherapeutic program for the treatment of a group of alcoholics (Crumbaugh, 1971). An effort was made to expand the perceptual awareness of these persons; for example, they were asked to look at the same picture on a variety of occasions in order to "see" it in a different way on each occasion. The researchers hoped that the subjects would thereby learn to "see" current and past life situations in a variety of ways and find new, alternative meanings in them. The researchers believed that such training would help these persons to transcend their egocentricity through increased interest in the potential meanings in the world. The scores on the Purpose-in-Life Test were reported to have increased after this training program.

This is one of the few reports of the effects of specific logotherapeutic procedures upon valuing fulfillment. A major weakness in this approach to valuing has been a lack of research on the effects of specific therapeutic/counseling procedures upon the sense of meaningfulness, purpose, and fulfillment.

The above research findings do lead to several general conclusions. People do differ in their fulfillment as valuers, and this difference can be measured. Individual differences in fulfillment as a valuer are related to psychological alienation and discomfort when fulfillment is low, and to self-confidence and interest in others when fulfillment is high. And, finally, training in skills that might facilitate specific forms of valuing may in fact increase the general sense of fulfillment in life.

THE ACTUALIZATION OF POTENTIAL: MASLOW

Abraham Maslow believed that the fulfillment of values occurs through the actualization of human potential, through the person becoming what he or she can be (Maslow, 1968, 1971). Maslow had already established his credentials as an American experimental psychologist when one day during the early 1940s he happened upon a patriotic children's parade; he reacted with such intense feeling that he decided that a new psychology was needed, a psychology based on the very best in human nature. He picked out certain persons he considered the best human beings, and he studied their psychological ways. Maslow came to believe the primary similarity among these persons centered in their being self-actualizing. They did not focus their energies upon making up for deficiencies but strove for growth into what they could be. Compared to most people, they had a clearer perception of reality, were more open to experience, were more unified and integrated, were spontaneous and expressive and identified and objective and democratic, and were able to love and to be creative.

Maslow described the moments of greatest self-actualization as peak-experiences, as moments of awareness that could be understood as fulfillment of being-values (or B-values, as he called them). These B-values, which define the nature of the fulfillment of the person's potential, include truth, goodness, beauty, unity, wholeness, aliveness, uniqueness, perfection, justice, order, simplicity, playfulness, effortlessness, meaningfulness, etc. Maslow considers these terms to be metaphors as they can only be defined by each other. Though each B-value occurs in the peak-experience and defines that experience in part, the peak-experience is more than any one or all of these B-values. It is a state of feeling, knowing, and being that one can truly identify only by pointing to it. Therefore, within the philosophy of science, the term *peak-experience* is a primitive term: it cannot truly be defined by words but only by pointing to instances. (Some of Maslow's writing approaches the mystical, in part because he was trying to describe in words something that was basically indescribable.) And, because the peak-experience is an inner psychological state, only the experiencer can point to his own experience.

Surprisingly, research on biofeedback – begun as an effort to reduce anxiety – has produced some evidence of distinctively physical states during meditation that are associated with peak-experience description (Ornstein, 1972). Though physiological correlates are evidence at a different level and hence are not the peak-experience itself, the existence of such instrumented data lends credence to the statements of peak-experiencers that they have lived through a psychological state that is truly different.

Maslow came to believe that B-values were *intrinsic* values, an instinctoid part of human biology, and were needed to avoid illness and to achieve healthy growth. The self-actualizing individual, however, does not seek the fulfillment of these values directly but through "some task, call, vocation, beloved work" outside the self. The person experiences values fulfillment, then, by forgetting the self and focusing upon some task involvement through which inner potential is expressed, thus becoming fully what he or she can be. The peak-experience, the moment of intense B-value awareness, occurs through transcending self by total involvement in a task "in the world."

Because B-values behave like needs, Maslow felt that the failure to experience them leads to *metapathologies* which require *metacounselors* who would aid persons to transcend themselves and thereby to actualize their potential. He also believed any "uncovering" type of psychotherapy was self-actualizing in that it revealed to the person his or her true nature, through insight into previously hidden inclinations.

To explore total involvement in a task, Tanzer (1968) undertook a comparative study of two groups of women — those who chose natural childbirth and those who selected the traditional physician-controlled method of delivery. As Tanzer examined the differences in psychological experience during delivery among the women in these two groups, she discovered a very interesting effect of the presence of the husband during delivery. Although not all women with husbands present during delivery reported peak-experiences, all those who *did* report such peak-experiences had their husbands present during the delivery. In addition to describing their peak-experiences with Maslow's B-value terms, the "husband-present-at-delivery" women more often described themselves as "Queenly, Blissful, Rapturous, Receptive, Victorious, Trusting, Joyful, Supreme, In-Ecstasy, Integrated" than did women whose husbands were not present. This study raises the question of why "good" medical practice defines human relationships in such a mechanical/instrumental way that husbands and wives must be separated during the birth process, thus depriving two persons of a moment of full humanness.

In order to assess individual levels of self-actualization, Shostrom (1966) created the Personal Orientation Inventory, which consists of 150 paired-comparison items. The respondent decides which of two alternatives "most consistently applies," for example, "a. I live by values which are in agreement with others. b. I live by values which are primarily based on my own feelings." Scores are obtained on two basic scales, Time Competence (Lives in the Present), and Inner Directed. These two scales are further subdivided into ten additional scales, two of which are described as Valuing scales. The Self-Actualizing Value scale is designed to assess the extent to which the respondent holds values of self-actualizing persons, and the Existentiality scale is designed to assess flexibility in the application of values.

Research involving the use of the Personal Orientation Inventory has proceeded along lines similar to the research on the Purpose-in-Life Test. First, persons nominated as self-actualizing by clinical psychologists produced higher scores as a group on the Self-Actualizing Values and Existentiality scales than did those nominated as nonactualizing (Shostrom, 1965). Second, high scores on the Self-Actualizing Value scale were significantly associated with high scores on the Identity Achievement Status Scale (Simmons, 1970); whereas high scores on the Existentiality scale were significantly associated with low scores on the F-scale for measuring authoritarianism and on the Rokeach scale for measuring dogmatic thinking (Dandes, 1966). Third, a group of persons who were just beginning psychotherapy scored lower on both the scales than did a group of persons who were in advanced stages of psychotherapy, having spent, an average of twenty-six months in therapy (Shostrom and Knapp, 1966).

These findings lead to several conclusions. Individual differences in level of self-actualization seem subject to assessment, and these differences are associated with the achievement of a sense of personal identity and with a democratic, nondogmatic orientation to social life. The differences in self-actualization between beginning and more advanced psychotherapy participants could be interpreted as validating psychotherapy as a means of increasing levels of self-actualization. That is, increased levels of values fulfillment may occur as one continues to discover oneself through psychotherapy – as proposed by Maslow himself.

ENHANCEMENT OF THE QUALITY
IN EXPERIENCE: CANTRIL

Hadley Cantril, an American social psychologist, was concerned with understanding our normal, everyday experiences of hope, fear, joy, sorrow, aspiration, or frustration. He could not accept the answers provided by theory and research on deviant and neurotic individuals, on conditioned responses, or on isolated sensory processes: "If we view man's behavior as a process of living we cannot be satisfied with a description of isolated aspects which neglect other aspects in the process and which merely relate the interaction of one variable with another" (Cantril, 1952). He concluded that the outstanding characteristic of the human is the capacity to sense the value quality in experience. The sense that an experience is worthwhile, satisfying, pleasant, fruitless, or disappointing he called the *value attribute* and observed that it occurs only in concrete situations. As every personal experience is pervaded by its own value quality, and as we remember the value qualities in past experiences, we begin to establish a standard or expectation of value quality that becomes our basis for judging each new experience. This acquired value standard, against which the worthwhileness of any life event is determined, is unique to each person, because it derives from the particular situations in which that person has participated. Hence, though there are no absolute units for the standard of value quality for all human beings, each person has his or her own quality units for such a standard.

The enhancement of the value quality in our experiencing is, according to Cantril, the ultimate and most generalizable goal of humans. Whether we sense ourselves to be fulfilled depends upon our success in enhancing the value quality in our experiencing. We try to recapture the value qualities we experienced on previous occasions, but this is rarely possible, first because situations never repeat themselves exactly and second because with repetition comes habituation and staleness.

Hence, in order to achieve a sense of value fulfillment through an increase in the quality of our experiences, we must seek out new situations and new goals. We experience increments in the value attribute when we overcome obstacles facing us in new situations, as we strive toward new goals. Yet, when we seek the new we risk losing the security, the certainty, we found in the old. Thus we constantly face choice, and this choice is between hope and fear — hope that if we do a new thing we will experience an emergent, increased value quality, and fear that we may lose even the old quality with which we could have been secure even though dulled through habituation. Thus the design of new ways of behaving in order to extend the range of value satisfactions is always an ambivalent effort, tinged with fears that the repeatability of previous value satisfactions will be lost. Hope and fear are a unit; when one is present so is the other. The aspirations of humans, from Cantril's vantage point, are inherently poignant.

Because the standard for judging value quality is based upon our experience in past situations, it follows that the standard itself may be developing. What may have been moderately enjoyable yesterday may be an exquisite delight today because of some intervening disaster. On the other hand, we may gradually increase our standard for what is an average satisfaction. The rate of change of this standard may well be a function of changes in our awareness of the range of potential satisfactions. For example, education itself might result in a rapidly decreasing sense of fulfillment as we become more and more aware of what we are not experiencing—even when our life situation has been quite stable and unchanging.

Two aspects of Cantril's theory influenced his research. The first is that each person develops his or her unique standard for the value quality of experience. The second is that this value quality is derived from actual previous life situations and anticipated events, including events occurring at the national level. Therefore, Cantril, as a research psychologist, was interested in measuring both the unique standard of the individual and that individual's perception of the status and fate of his nation (Cantril, 1965). Through such measurement he hoped to gain insight into the genesis of aspirations as a function of national events, into how the value fulfillment of an individual was related to his perception of the development of the nation.

As a tool for such research Cantril created, with F. Kilpatrick, the Self-Anchoring Striving Scale (Kilpatrick and Cantril, 1960). A respondent is presented with a device that looks like a ladder. Numbers, ranging from 0 to 10, are placed between the rungs of the ladder, and the respondent is asked to describe the top "anchoring" number (10) as the wishes and hopes which, if fulfilled, would constitute the "best possible life." The bottom "anchoring" number (0) is described by the respondent as the worries and fears embodied in the conception of the worst possible life imaginable. The respondent is then asked to indicate the rung where he believes he stands now, where he stood at some specific time in the past, and where he anticipates standing at some specified time in the future. The past and future dates in Cantril's research were both five years from the present. To gain insight into the respondents' perspectives on national development, Cantril also used the ladder scale to ask each respondent to define his or her highest hopes and greatest fears for the nation and then to indicate on the ladder the nation's status currently, five years in the past, and antici- pated five years in the future.

The Self-Anchoring Striving Scale was administered to citizens of some thirteen nations differing in level of development during the late 1950s and early 1960s; it produced an extensive range of data on hopes and fears for self and for nation (Cantril, 1965). Only a few illustrative findings can be provided here:

1. Among United States citizens the average ladder rating for self in the present was 6.6, for five years in the past 5.9, and for five years in the future 7.8. The same ratings for the nation were 6.7, 6.5, and 7.4, suggesting that personal value fulfillment in the United States was judged to be at about the same level as national development — present, past, and future.

2. The data from all nations were consistent in that the ratings in- creased as one moved from the past through the present to the future. The average person thought the present was better than the past and anticipated that the future would be better than the present.

3. When citizens of a nation mentioned many hopes, they also men- tioned many fears — the sheer volume of concerns that provide the foundation for fulfillment differs from nation to nation. A rise in aspiration that comes with newly recognized possibilities also seems to carry with it a multitude of fears.

4. Those concerns that people used to define hopes and fears for themselves centered around their personal economic situation, their family, and their health, while national concerns centered around

general economic conditions, internal political stability, and the potential for international conflict. Interestingly enough, such matters as emotional stability and success at work were mentioned by only 13 to 14 percent of the respondents as a basis for their personal hopes and fears; concerns related to social justice were mentioned by only 21 percent as a basis for their hopes and fears for their own nation. Hence, the value quality of experience, as far as this research accurately assesses it, seemingly depends upon judgments of economic development and social stability, both within the personal realm and within the national realm.

Cantril emphasized that the concerns of people seemed patterned largely according to the phase of the development of their nation, and he proposed five such phases. Each characterizes the main body of the citizens of a nation; there are always subgroups whose development is behind or ahead of the majority's. Phase One is described by Cantril as *acquiescence to circumstances.* Many citizens of India simply were unable to respond to the ladder scale, as they seemed to have no definable better or worse conditions for living. Some rural Brazilians and Filipinos, as disadvantaged subgroups, were so concerned about simple survival needs that the possibility of aspiration to a higher quality of value satisfaction was not a reality for them. During Phase Two an *awakening to potentialities* occurs. In this phase people become aware of possibilities for increasing the range and extent of their satisfactions and realize that life experiences can have an emergent quality. During Phase Three comes *knowledge of the means to realize goals.* In this phase, the greatest national instability occurs. As aspirations awaken, citizens become impatient with slow progress in the development of practical technologies and/or social institutions for the implementation of new means to satisfaction. Phase Four brings a new *experiencing of intended consequences through action,* and Phase Five is characterized by *a general satisfaction with a way of life that promises continued development.*

The value fulfillment of individuals thus seems to be derived from their own life history, their awareness of potentialities outside their own life sphere, and their capacity to implement their hopes as judged by the phase of development of their nation-state. It can also be concluded from Cantril's research that people are creatures of optimism who, regardless of their current level of value fulfillment, anticipate an increment in value quality in the future.

THE EMERGENCE OF RESEARCH ON
THE QUALITY OF LIFE

During the 1960s in the United States, faith in the perpetual growth of industrialization as a means of meeting human needs came into question with the recognition that smog, water pollution, cancer, etc., are by-products of such industrialization. People became aware that many of the less obvious effects of apparently desirable processes were reducing rather than increasing the quality of the environment and thereby the quality of life experiences. Government programs were developed to assess the social impact of a wide range of components in societal organizations, including the impact of the government's own programs. The term given to the evaluation of the impact of government programs is *Social Impact Assessment,* and the data gathered for such impact assessments are called *social indicators.* Social indicators are defined as objective characteristics of communities that can be described through census data, for example, the infant mortality rate, the robbery rate, the suicide rate, the unemployment rate, air pollution levels, and, on the positive side, levels of contribution to the United Fund.

During the late 1970s some social scientists began to express some uneasiness about the validity of these objective indicators as measures of the goodness of life. Mark Schneider (1976), writing in the *Public Administration Review,* said, "It is arguable that actual individual welfare and the quality of life actually experienced by people is a more highly subjective condition than implied by descriptive social indicators." If the quality of life lies in the *experience* of life, then social indicators are only "surrogate indicators"; they describe the conditions of life that might be assumed to influence life experiences, but they do not assess these experiences directly.

Several research projects are currently under way to study the subjective quality of life. Schneider (1976) designed a study to assess the relationship of the subjective experience to the objective indicators. Blau (1977), using an evaluation research approach, identified ten aspects of the quality of life mentioned by persons undergoing psychotherapy that could be used to evaluate the impact of therapy on their lives. The most extensive and intensive study of the nature of the subjective quality of life yet undertaken, however, is that of Flanagan (1978) at the American Institutes for Research. This research is a continuation of Project Talent, probably the most ambitious survey of the development of national human resources ever undertaken. It was directed toward (1) the inductive creation of a classification scheme for indicators of the subjective quality of life, and (2) an analysis of how the level of satisfaction in each area contributes to the overall subjective quality of life.

The study conducted by the American Institutes for Research was administered to nearly three thousand people of various ages, races, and socioeconomic backgrounds, representing all regions of the nation. They were asked to provide "critical incidents" in response to questions that included the following:

> Think of the last time you did something very important to you or had an experience that was especially satisfying to you. What did you do or what happened that was so satisfying to you? Why did this experience seem so important or satisfying? Think of a time you saw something happen to a person that really was harmful or made their life worse in some way. Exactly what happened to this person? Why do you feel this made their life worse? What should have happened to this person?

Some sixty-five hundred critical incidents, actual events that were judged to have created satisfaction or to have made life worse, were described in response to the research questions. These descriptions were sorted and re-sorted by research staff into categories of events involving similarities in behavior and experience, and the categories were finally refined into a set of fifteen:

1. Material well-being and financial security (having good food, a home, possessions, or comforts)
2. Health and personal safety (enjoying freedom from sickness or possessing physical and mental fitness)

3. Relations with spouse (or girl or boy friend) (love, companionship, sexual satisfaction)

4. Having and raising children (becoming a parent, watching children develop, guiding and helping)

5. Relations with parents, siblings, or other relatives (visiting, enjoying, sharing, understanding, being helped by and helping them)

6. Relations with friends (having good friends, being accepted, sharing, providing support and guidance)

7. Activities related to helping or encouraging other people (church, club, or volunteer group that works for the benefit of other people)

8. Activities related to local and national government (keeping informed, voting, appreciating political and social and religious freedom, having living conditions governed by regulations)

9. Intellectual development (learning, improving understanding in and out of school)

10. Personal understanding and planning (developing and gaining orientation, purpose, and guiding principles for one's life, personal maturity and growth)

11. Occupational role (having interesting, rewarding, worthwhile work in a job or at home, including doing well and using one's abilities)

12. Creativity and personal expression (showing ingenuity or originality or imagination in arts or crafts, practical or scientific matters, including expressing oneself through a collection, a personal project or an accomplishment)

13. Socializing (entertaining, attending parties, meeting new people)

14. Passive and observational activities (watching television, listening to music, reading, going to sporting events)

15. Active and participating recreational activities (sports, vacation travel, dancing)

Each of these fifteen aspects was submitted to a nationally representative age cohort of one thousand persons who, when they were fifteen years old in 1960, had participated in the original data collection for Project Talent. When the current data were collected in 1975, the participants were approximately thirty years of age. In addition, six hundred persons aged fifty and six hundred persons aged seventy served as research respondents. The respondents were asked to rate the importance to them of each of the fifteen aspects defining the quality of life. The five-point scale ranged from very important through important, moderately important, and slightly important to not at all important. They were also asked to rate on another five-point scale how well their needs and wants were being met. The scale ranged from very well through well, moderately well, only slightly well to not at all well.

The resulting data indicated that the needs and wants of most persons were well met in the areas most important to their quality of life and that the three age cohorts, as well as both men and women, showed strikingly similar responses. Over 80 percent of the persons of all ages and both sexes indicated that health and personal safety, having and raising children, and understanding themselves were very important. All the groups also agreed about which aspects were detracting from the quality of life, in which their needs and wants were *not* being met, to wit, participating in local and national government, learning, participating in active recreation, and expressing themselves in a creative manner.

Two special analyses were made of the responses of the fifty-year-old and the seventy-year-old groups. They were asked to rate the overall quality of their lives, and this rating was correlated with the degree to which each of the needs and wants was being fulfilled. The six areas that showed the highest relationship between fulfillment and overall quality of life were material comforts, health, work, active recreation, learning, and creative expression.

The second study was a factor analysis of the fifteen aspects. The first factor consisted of the material comfort, work, and health aspects. The second factor involved fulfillment of the socializing and close friends aspects, and the third factor centered on fulfillment of learning and creative expression. A comparison of these two sets of findings suggests that the overall quality of life for Americans is based on fulfillment of career-related and avocational activities but not on friendships or relationships.

Flanagan concluded that experienced social scientists could make objective and reliable estimates regarding an individual's present needs and the effects of specific social programs upon that individual's overall quality of life. This point of view seems a direct, contemporary expression of the orientation of Cantril, having its roots in the desire to tie personal fulfillment to national circumstances and policy. Considering the current world situation, the potential for continuing research along these lines seems great, especially in comparison to the potential for research based on the ideas of Frankl (who emphasized finding meaning in suffering) and those of Maslow (who emphasized transcending adjustment). These latter approaches seem to have stimulated more discussion and literary expression than research.

The Invitation to Express Slighted Values

The end of the last chapter described a process whereby people were allowed to identify their own uniquely organized value systems. When this process is included in the program known as the Values Exploration Workshop (Simmons, 1978), there is a further assignment. Participants identify their thirteen most important values from a set of one hundred values presented and then are requested to rank-order these values according to the extent to which each is clearly expressed in their behavior. The three lowest-ranked values are then labelled "the least actualized of your most important values." The participants are then given the assignment of developing a way to express each of these values in action during each day of the next week.

The responses to this assignment have been informative. First, some people are strongly committed to values that simply cannot be expressed in action at a given time, for example, the unmarried nineteen-year-old who values "having happy, healthy children." In such a case the commitment itself is significant and sufficient for a sense of value fulfillment. This is quite consistent with Frankl's position. Second, when some persons try to express a value in action, they find that they had misestimated its significance to them — "I guess I really don't give a damn about that. It sounded nice, but there doesn't seem to be any way I can get involved in expressing that value." In addition, actual experience with fulfilling values may have a feedback effect upon the value system itself, bringing about change.

Related to the above points is the example of two women who have grown children living independently. One places "having happy, healthy children" in her highest category of values and the other places the same value in her lowest category. One says, "My children are gone from my home, but that is still one of my cherished values"; the other says, "That part of my life is over and done, and I'm now much more involved with other values." The implication here is that the value systems of some persons operate as "eternal ideals," which do not change regardless of fulfillment, while other value systems operate as "immediate aspirations," in which values, when fulfilled, drop out to be replaced by new aspirations. In one case commitment is sufficient to establish and maintain a value system, while in another case the system responds structurally to feedback.

Another observed effect of the assignment was some participants' self-congratulation at the expression of their values. They discovered that "setting their minds to doing something" did in fact lead to a greater sense of fulfillment, whether they chose to establish a regular exercise pattern to implement "having good health" or (the response of a Hungarian expatriate) wrote the Russian Embassy in London to say it was none of the Russian government's business whether the British sold Harrier airplanes to the Chinese. Values fulfillment may involve a sense of effort, and it may even be the effort itself rather than the results that brings the sense of vitality and fulfillment. There can be great personal pride in writing a letter even though one knows that it may have little effect. Value efforts can in fact be fulfilling even when they have a negative personal effect, for, as Frankl clearly points out, humans will die for their values.

A final aspect of the assignment in values expression carries a further implication regarding the differences among the three approaches to valuing fulfillment presented in this chapter. Some people identify as their most important values those that are similar to the Cantril and Flanagan type of categories, for example, "establishing and maintaining a career for myself." Others select values much more along the lines of

Maslow's B-values, for example, "simplicity," "being myself"; and still others emphasize a Franklian "accepting circumstances for what they are." Could it be that each of these three approaches to values fulfillment reflects attention to a specific and distinctive type of valuer? Each of the three orientations may be quite valid, appropriately applied. What would be needed, then, would be some criteria for selecting the appropriate approach for each person.

SUMMARY

Values fulfillment has been variously proposed to be a matter of commitment, of action, of actualizing potential, of transcending self, of increased satisfaction resulting from improved living conditions, of finding meaning regardless of circumstances, and more. Frankl proposed that man's primary motivation is the search for meaning, which is found through values. Research with the Purpose-in-Life Test, derived from Frankl's theory, indicates that the failure to find meaning is associated with psychological alienation and discomfort. Maslow proposed that one experiences values fulfillment in and through B-values during moments when one's potential as a human is most fully expressed. Research with the Personal Orientation Inventory suggests that people who are self-actualizing have a higher sense of personal identity and a more democratic, nondogmatic orientation to living. Cantril proposed that every experience in life has a value quality, and human beings seek an increase in the value quality in their experiences. His research on the relationship between personal and national hopes and fears finds a contemporary counterpart in Flanagan's attempts to identify the aspects of living that contribute to the subjective evaluation of the quality of life.

Simmons asked individuals to express slighted values, and their reported experience had several implications. One was that values fulfillment may be a different process for different people.

5.

Valuing Competence and Valuing Skills

Is ONE VALUE JUDGMENT just as correct as another? The man in the street tends to classify as value judgments those that he apparently makes out of personal preference, without supporting justification. With no real justification, one value judgment is as good as another, and value judgment becomes a matter of taste.

In contrast to this conception of value judgments are the ideas of the classical moral philosophers, such as Plato and Kant, and of three modern theorists, Robert Hartman, Lawrence Kohlberg, and John Dewey. Although these modern scholars differ greatly among themselves, they all believe that choices based upon value judgments are the product of psychological processing and, further, that skills in making better or more correct value judgments can be developed. From this vantage point, some value judgments are better than others, and it becomes reasonable to believe that through the educational process the valuer can learn to be more competent in formulating a value judgment and in making choices based on such judgment.

THE EMERGENCE OF A SECULAR ORIENTATION TO VALUES EDUCATION

For decades, popular ideology in the United States held that the nation was a great melting pot of persons from all over the world, in which the best values, brought by these people, merged into a unified and shared system. During the 1960s, however, this assumption was challenged. It was asserted that the "mainstream" value system was in fact not a merged, shared-value system, but the system of that group which held power, the white, Anglo-Saxon, Protestant class—the so-called WASP group. Hence, what purported to be a value-free educational system was now identified as an educational system designed to promote the values of the group with the most power. Meanwhile, other value systems were actually guiding the lives of various groups of persons.

This challenge to the exclusive legitimacy of WASP values led to an increased awareness about values education. The flood of educational materials and packages on values education being promoted by publishers in the 1970s can best be understood as one expression of the emergence of a values education movement with a secular base.

Because there was so much variety in the materials being promoted as values education teaching units, the Social Science Education Consortium (funded by the National Institute of Education, itself a division of the United States Department of Health, Education and Welfare) produced a catalog of available materials classified according to a system created by the senior author. This catalog, the *Values Education Sourcebook* (Superka et al., 1976), had five main categories: (1) materials directed toward the inculcation of certain values, (2) materials directed toward aiding the person to clarify his or her own value commitments, (3) materials directed toward enhancing the individual's effectiveness in acting upon values already held dear, (4) materials fostering development in "moral judgment," and (5) materials directed toward developing intellectual skills for the analysis of value problems. This classification scheme seems harmonious with the three aspects of valuing proposed in this book, though a review of the packages that were available suggests a heavy weighting toward the development of valuing competence.

Before we turn to the theoretical approaches to the nature of valuing competence, we should note the existence of an orientation to values education that emphasizes the logic of evidence as the basis for value judgments. *Values Education: Rationale, Strategies, and Procedures* was published in 1971 as the 41st Yearbook of the National Council for the Social Studies. The central theme of this yearbook was that values education is teaching people how to evaluate the adequacy of a values-based statement, such as "Nixon was a good president." The proposed evaluative decision-making process involves six steps: (1) identifying and clarifying the value question, (2) assembling (gathering and organizing) purported facts, (3) assessing the truth of the purported facts, (4) clarifying the relevance of the facts, (5) arriving at a tentative value decision, and (6) testing the value principle implied in the decision. This is primarily a "balance sheet" approach to conflict resolution, and its reliance upon evidence reveals it to be essentially an *empirical* approach to value judgment. As such, it is readily adaptable to the traditional educational procedures in U.S. schools, which emphasize "getting the facts." The way to deal with value choices, then, is to get the evidence ("the facts"); the evidence will then decide for you.

The main alternatives to this empirical approach are the *intuitive*—having faith in your inner human sense of what is correct regardless of facts or reason—and the *rational*—relying upon pure logic within a system of concepts to determine the correct judgment. This book does not present the intuitive notion that each person has a "built-in crap-detector." Robert Hartman in his writings best presents the rational approach in his identification of the basic axiom for a science of value and his further derivation of a whole system for evaluating the adequacy of value choices on the basis of this one axiom.

THE SCIENCE OF VALUE: HARTMAN

Robert Hartman was a philosopher whose early life was spent in Germany and Sweden but whose professional life centered in the United States and Mexico. His primary interest in philosophy was in the nature of "good" and of "goodness" (Hartman, 1959, 1967). He came to believe that his fellow philosophers were stuck with what appeared to be an intuitive basis for defining goodness, and he maintained that he had discovered a rational way for them to get unstuck.

He took his intellectual predecessor to be the British philosopher G. E. Moore, and he considered Moore's major contribution to be the definition of the "naturalistic fallacy." Moore had concluded essentially that "though good is what it is and not another thing, it is not, in itself, a good thing." What it is, unfortunately, Moore did not know. Stated a little less whimsically, goodness is that which all good things have in common; however, this goodness does not have the same thing in common with all good things as they do with each other. The dilemma centered around two propositions held to be true by Moore (and elaborated by Hartman): (1) goodness is not a natural property of a thing, and yet (2) the goodness of a thing depends upon its natural properties. Hartman provides an example of this distinction. If you tell a person, "I have a good car," the person will know much about that car—it has an engine that runs, brakes that brake, tires that are not flat, and doors that open. He will know nothing, however, about the particular natural properties of your car: its color, the number of cylinders in the motor, whether it has two or four doors, or its interior style. In other words, he knows the relationship of your car to the concept "car," but he knows nothing of your car's specific properties. If you tell this person to go outside and find your car, he cannot do so because he does not know what it looks like, what are its natural properties. Still, the goodness of your car depends upon its natural properties. To confuse these natural properties of a thing with its goodness is to commit the naturalistic fallacy.

Hartman's resolution to Moore's dilemma is that goodness is not a property of *things* but of *concepts*. To know a thing will tell you nothing of its goodness. To know that something is good requires that you know the concept of which the thing is an instance. This recognition led Hartman to propose that the basic axiom for a science of value (and the solution to the problem of the naturalistic fallacy) is that *a thing is good when it fulfills the definition of its concept.*

The nature of valuing competency then becomes a matter of (1) not committing the naturalistic fallacy, i.e., not confusing the properties of a thing with its fulfillment of the definition of the concept against which it is judged, and (2) knowing concepts, i.e., "One can value a thing only if one knows its name [implying its ideal qualities] and its [actual] properties." A given object is neither good nor bad in itself but only as an instance of a concept. Take, for example, an object manufactured for sale as a chair. It may well be a good chair, but most likely it will not be a good ironing board. The goodness of a thing is a function of the concept applied to it, its "name" and the properties in that concept.

Hartman elaborated in considerable detail the theoretical system derived from his basic axiom. For instance, some goodnesses are better than others. To understand this conclusion, one must know first that the properties of a concept are referred to as its intensions. A chair has a seat, legs constructed so as to hold the seat stable, etc., and the value of a single chair is the degree to which it satisfies these intensions. One chair, thus, may be more valuable than another because it fulfills more intensions. Now it also follows that some concepts have more intensions than others. The complete fulfillment of one concept may be better than the complete fulfillment of another because the first concept has more intensions that can be fulfilled; that is, the more intensions an instance can fulfill, the more goodness potential it has.

Hartman proposes three standards of value judgment, which are in fact three types of concepts, each with its own language and number of intensions. A *synthetic concept* (1) is a "mental construct," an idea; (2) has a definite number of intensions that can be counted; and (3) uses technical language—a circle is a mathematical construct with a few highly specific properties that are described in its formula (the technical language). An *analytic concept* (1) involves an abstraction from events, (2) has an infinity of potential intensions that can be counted, and (3) can be discussed with ordinary language—a social role, for example, is an abstract notion that has its roots in concrete behavior and may have a multitude of components, which, however, may be counted. A *singular concept* (1) is the proper name of an individual, (2) has an infinite number of intensions that are nondenumerable, and (3) its language is the metaphor, e.g., Spot is the name of one dog, and although there are an infinite number of ways in which he can be himself, we cannot count them but can only say, "Isn't he being a peach today?" meaning, of course, that he is really being true to his own nature.

These three types of concepts lead to three types of value categories: (1) the *systemic*, which usually refers to ideas, (2) the *extrinsic*, which usually refers to things, and (3) the *intrinsic*, which usually refers to individual persons. These three categories differ in the number of intensions that each can fulfill. Thus the fulfillment of an intrinsic concept results in more value than the fulfillment of an extrinsic concept, which in turn has more value than the fulfillment of a systemic concept. Any individual person has more value than any object, which in turn is of more value than an idea. Those who do not so value, those who will sacrifice persons and things for an idea, we refer to as fanatics.

By adding sawdust to chocolate pudding we can decrease the value of the pudding. By adding whipped cream to chocolate pudding, we can increase the value of the pudding. When concepts are combined in more complex and mixed categories, the increase or decrease in value becomes more difficult to calculate. An effort to solve such problems led to the *axiological calculus*, through which the number of terms in the intension of combinations can be established. This calculus was considered by Hartman to be an exact science. Suffice it to be considered here a rational, deductively established procedure for determining the worth of instances.

This, then, provides the third foundation stone for valuing competency—that of recognizing the relative number of intensions in the concepts that are being used to evaluate instances and events. Knowing the number of intensions puts one in the position of knowing the relative goodness of two alternatives about which a judgment must be made.

Hartman believed that before we ask a person to select his or her values, as the Rokeach and Morris surveys do, we need to know that person's capacity for making value judgments in general. Commitment to certain values when one's judgment is poor could possibly lead to frustration and a failure to develop a sense of fulfillment—as well as to instability of commitment.

To assess this value judgment capacity, he created the Hartman Value Profile (Hartman, 1973), which has two parts. On Part A the respondent finds eighteen concepts that refer to the external world—"a good meal," "nonsense," "slavery," "a short circuit," or "a baby." He or she is requested to rank-order these concepts from the best to the worst. On Part B the respondent again finds eighteen concepts to be ranked from best to worst, but these refer to the respondent — "I like my work, it does me good," "No matter how hard I work, I shall always feel frustrated," and "My life is messing up the world."

Both sets of concepts have theoretically correct ranks based on the axiological calculus of intensional complexity, and a variety of indices have been created for assessing different aspects of valuing competency. These include such aspects of competency as "the development of the capacity to differentiate values in general within the world and within the self," "the development of the capacity for organizing one's reactions when confronted with value problems within the world and within the self," "the development of the capacity to distinguish between the good and the bad in the outside world and within oneself," "the development of the ability to value accurately oneself as a person," and "the development of the ability to discern the important within the complex in situations concerning one's role in the world."

The promise of Hartman's theory as a basis for facilitating individual valuing competency is just a promise at this time. The manual for his value profile was published posthumously, and efforts to implement his ideas are only now beginning through the formation of a society dedicated to him (The R.S. Hartman Institute for Formal and Applied Axiology).

One early beginning was the Austin and Van Arkel (1973) study of persons imprisoned in a local jail, begun with the notion that such persons may well be there because of valuational deficiencies. That is, they may be victims of their lack of capacity to differentiate between the good and the bad in the world, resulting in failure to make proper value judgments. Although much research needs to be done along this line, the potential for rehabilitation of certain types of offenders seems striking. Hartman has presented a complex system for the diagnosis of valuational capacity that could also be converted into an educational process for teaching people who make poor value judgments how to improve the quality of their judgments.

The Development of Principled Moral Judgment: Kohlberg

Lawrence Kohlberg, an American developmental social psychologist, was curious about how children thought about value conflicts and how they reasoned through conflicting claims between people. To study this reasoning he created a variety of moral dilemmas and presented them to children with the request that they recommend a solution. One of the most widely repeated dilemmas is that of "Heinz and the Drug." Heinz's wife is dying from cancer, and he learns that a druggist has discovered a cure for this cancer. But, the druggist is charging more money for the drug than Heinz can raise. The question posed to the children is, Should Heinz steal the drug? And, if so or not so, why or why not? Kohlberg (1958) classified into three major types the various rationales used by children to justify the course of action they recommended:

1. Heinz should be guided by potential consequences to himself—"He shouldn't steal the drug because he could be put in jail."
2. Heinz should be guided by community norms and conventions—"Heinz shouldn't steal the drug because it is against the law."
3. Heinz should be guided by a universal principle—"Heinz should steal the drug because no law should ever be made that would deprive someone of his right to live just so someone else can make some money."

Kohlberg further proposed (1969, 1971a, 1971b, 1973) that these types of response actually reflect universal levels of judgment in moral valuing—these levels are culture-free. The developing individual moves through these levels in invariant sequence and at the highest level, relies upon principles of justice as the basis for decision making. (One such principle is that one's own rights should always be balanced against the rights of others.) Justice, then, is the value that provides the standard for the highest level of decision making.

The notion that laws of human development require every person to move through levels of reasoning in a never varying sequence was elaborated by Kohlberg in his six-stage theory. He traces reasoning about moral dilemmas through six stages, two stages occurring at each of three general levels. Level One is referred to as *Premoral* or *Preconventional* thinking. Its first stage is Stage One — *Punishment and obedience orientation*, during which one reasons that one should obey rules in order to avoid pain and punishment. It also includes Stage Two — *Naive instrumental hedonism*, during which one reasons that one should conform in order to obtain rewards and have favors returned.

Level Two reasoning is referred to as *Morality of conventional role conformity*. It includes Stage Three — *Good boy/good girl morality of maintaining positive relations with, and approval by, others*, during which one reasons that one should conform to community expectations in order to avoid dislike and disapproval by others. Also at this level is Stage Four — *Authority maintaining morality*, during which one reasons that one should behave in certain ways in order to maintain rules of an orderly society and legitimate authority.

Level Three is referred to as *Morality of self-accepted moral principles*. Its first stage is Stage Five — *Morality of contract of individual rights and of democratically accepted law*, during which one reasons that one should honor one's personal contracts and should maintain the respect of an impartial spectator judging in terms of community welfare. The final stage, Stage Six — is *Morality of individual principles of conscience*, during which one reasons that one's duty is to avoid self-condemnation.

These stages involve an increasing degree of internalization of moral standards and result in a reorganization of perspective about the meaning of culturally universal values. For example, the meaning of the individual human life is reinterpreted at each stage in terms of the level of reasoning emphasized at that level. Stated in a slightly different way, the meaning a person assigns to a value is influenced by his or her level of reasoning about social conflicts; one's value judgments are always screened through one's current level of thinking about conflicting claims. The expression of one's value system is influenced by the meaning of the values in that system in light of one's current reasoning about the nature of obligation.

Kohlberg (1968) suggested that the three general levels of moral reasoning are somewhat analogous to three major philosophical theories about the development of morality. The British Utilitarians (Hume, 1751; Smith, 1759; Mill, 1861) supported the theory that acts are judged good or bad on the basis of their consequences; hence, the right choice is the one that brings the greatest good for the greatest number. This "preconventional" basis for rightness is contrasted with the "conventional" theory of Durkheim (1961). He proposed a sociological analysis of morality that supported the notion that morals are based upon group norms; that is, the psychological origins of morality grow out of the individual's respect for his or her group and for the authorities who represent the group. Morals, then, are relative to group membership.

The third, or justice-based, level of reasoning is represented by Piaget (1932). In his analysis of the basis for the rules for playing marbles, he generated the idea of an emergent moral capacity through which the child rises above his or her initial "egocentricity" and "realism" to recognize that rules are not the result of consequences or group authority but are the outgrowth of social contract. Morality, in this view, stems from the capacity to understand the natural conditions of social relationships and to see that justice is the primary principle that guides the resolution of social dilemmas.

Kohlberg believed that all three levels of rationale could be found in the reasoning of children at different stages and that his theory was an elaboration upon Piaget's position. However, he also makes clear that he does not hold the development of moral thinking to be a simple unfolding of innate forms of thought structure. Rather, the developments in thought occur as a natural consequence of the child's being faced with dilemmas of social living and, further, being required to resolve them in some fashion. (And Kohlberg does not believe there is any research evidence to support Piaget's suggestion that the emergence of peer-based rule-setting in the ten-to-thirteen age bracket indicates that preference for democratic political forms is an innate psychological characteristic of man as a social animal.)

Each person passes through each stage, in order and independent of culture, and understands all moral arguments at or below the current personal stage as well as the next stage up. Kohlberg suggests, in fact, that people will tend to prefer the arguments based on the logic of the next stage up from the current one. Because of this, he indicates that moral education should consist of the presentation of dilemmas during which arguments are prepared at the present stage of the discussants and at one stage above the current one. In this way a discussant is exposed to arguments consistent with a higher level of reasoning than his or her current level and, being naturally attracted to a more advanced level of argument, will personally adopt this next stage. This process, according to Kohlberg, leads persons to higher levels of reasoning but does not inculcate specific solutions; moral education is not designed to promote or teach specific conventions in ideology or behavior. For example, Heinz may be encouraged to steal the drug because if his wife dies he will be punished or, in contrast, he will be advised not to steal the drug because he will be sent to jail if he's caught. The level of reasoning (Stage One) does not incline toward any specific solution, despite the reader's hidden assumption that moral reasoning necessarily leads to the more humane solution.

Humaneness, being loving and forgiving, is not the criterion for the highest level of moral reasoning either. The two formal criteria for the highest level of moral judgment are *universality* and *prescriptivity*. The highest level of moral reasoning, based upon the principle of justice, is a way of thinking about competing claims of real people in real situations and involves basing any solution on two assumptions: (1) that the competitors should be treated as moral equals (the solution would not change if the competitors changed places; it would be applied "regardless of who it was") and (2) that the solution would be constructed as a prescriptive course of action in one specific situation (the solution is not a rule or general commandment or practice; it would be applied only once).

When developing an educational practice to apply Kohlberg's model as a means of increasing valuing competence, one should include three components. First, in order to arouse genuine moral conflict or uncertainty, one must present a dilemma or challenging issue that is particularly gripping. Second, one must present arguments that express modes of thought at the current stage of development and the next stage up. Third, discussion should occur among peers assisted by the educator, whose responsibility is to see that contrasting arguments are presented and pursued. Blatt and Kohlberg (1973) applied just such a procedure, and their results indicate that the process does help move children from one stage to the next.

To assess individual differences in principled moral judgment, Kohlberg constructed a structured interview during which a respondent is presented with a series of dilemmas, such as the Heinz problem or what to do when an escaped convict who has established himself as a model citizen in the years since his escape is recognized and the respondent is faced with the question of whether or not to turn him in. The expressed reasoning given for the solution to the dilemma is then scored for level of development.

Recently, Rest et al. (Rest, 1974; Rest, Cooper, Coder, and Masanz, 1974) objectified the scoring for principled moral judgment through the creation of a paper-and-pencil instrument, the Defining Issues Test. This test also presents dilemmas, but the respondent, rather than giving his own solutions, is asked to rate the relative importance of each of a series of issues to the resolution of a given dilemma. Each of the issues, except for a nonsense issue, represents the concern of one of the Kohlbergian stages. Test scores indicate the ability of the person to recognize the central importance of higher-level issues involved in the resolution of a dilemma, in contrast to lower-level or even nonsense issues. Presumably, the higher one's scores, the greater should be one's competence to make correct value judgments and choices when faced with moral value dilemmas in daily life.

Though there are differences between Kohlberg's interview-based research orientation and the orientation underlying the Defining Issues Test, scores from the two approaches show a high correlation (Rest, 1976; Rest, Davison and Robbins, 1978). One interesting finding by Panowitsch (1975) was that students increased their scores on the Defining Issues Test following a course in ethics but such an increase was not found following a course in logic. The implication of this finding is that knowledge about how to think logically is not the same as competence in identifying the importance of issues to the resolution of dilemmas in moral valuing.

Because he believed that level of moral judgment was content-free, not influenced by any specific values, Kohlberg classified himself on one occasion as a deontologist. The use of principled moral thinking to solve a moral conflict does not predestine any particular solution to the dilemma; moral thinking is a process that does not prejudice the outcome of any problem. As one reads Kohlberg's writings, however, one cannot help but be reminded of Sahakian's (1968) comment that some philosophers do not believe the good and the right can be separated. To Kohlberg, justice is a way of thinking about competing claims of real people in real situations. To others, the author included, justice is a value, an end state that serves as a standard for behavior and thought. Further study of Kohlberg's ideas may clarify the relationship between what is right and what is worthwhile.

VALUATION SKILLS: DEWEY AND THE VALUES CLARIFICATION GROUP

John Dewey was an American, psychologically oriented philosopher who was reputed to be a pragmatist. When he turned his attention to valuing during the late 1930s, he concluded that valuational phenomena consist of (1) an unsatisfactory existing condition, (2) a more satisfactory prospective situation, and (3) activities that lead from the unsatisfactory to the satisfactory condition (Dewey, 1939). Thus, valuing and value behavior arise within specific, concrete, real-life situations; and although value issues involve deficit or conflict, the resolution of a value problem is accomplished through the achievement of a positive solution. Reasonable values, to Dewey, were those that, after some thought, seemed capable of achievement. Dewey emphasized the thought given to value problems in order to point out that valuation (as he referred to all valuing activity) always involved an intellectual factor, the *factor of inquiry.*

The measure of the value a person attaches to a given end is not what is said about its preciousness but the care devoted to obtaining and using the means without which the end could not be obtained. Valuing is a matter of *caring for and looking after,* or fostering, the means by which ends-in-view are to be attained. Dewey was very concerned about the distinction between *end states,* which were accomplished, and *ends-in-view,* which were the plans one hoped would be achieved through effort. He emphasized that his conception of valuing as goal oriented was not teleological; the future does not determine the present activity. It is the present ends-in-view that propel the valuer into the future. Effort does not arise out of desire, but effort and desire are the same because, as noted above, what one values *is* what one does to achieve goals.

A central valuing activity is *careful consideration,* which involves both (1) the adequacy of inquiry into the lacks and deficits in an existing situation and (2) the adequacy of inquiry into the likelihood that a given end-in-view will in fact resolve the unsatisfactory situation through fulfilling the need or through resolving a conflict. Dewey believed that means could not be separated from the ends toward which they were directed and, also, that ends can become means and so on in a continuing flow of events. There is thus a need to foresee all the effects of one mean-end structure upon other mean-end structures. One must give due regard to the effects of one valuational solution upon other aspects of living. When one considers the use of DDT to control insects, one must also consider additional effects of such a means upon other things, such as birdlife. Valuing does not consist of simply making decisions one at a time; it involves a continuing process and is part of a complex stream of events. The merit of different ends, as well as different means, must be estimated according to their apparent capacity to make good existing lacks or resolve existing conflicts.

Dewey's emphasis upon valuation as a task-oriented, problem-solving, and intellectually guided activity has been restated by a group of educators who collectively refer to their approach to valuing as Values Clarification (e.g., Raths, Harmin, and Simon, 1966). These educators propose that the reason that children are apathetic or uncertain or flighty or inconsistent or drifting or overconforming or overdissenting or phony is that they lack clarity in their relationship to society. Those who have such clarity are described as purposeful, positive, enthusiastic, proud; yet they are not "adjusted" to society in any passive sense. The common malady of those who lack clarity is their confusion over values, while those who have clarity possess a set of beliefs about themselves in relation to society that is (1) extensive in scope, (2) dependable in action, and (3) internally compatible.

Faced with the task of identifying what processes might be effective in aiding young people to obtain values – those general guides that give direction to life – the Values Clarification group began by defining a value as something that satisfies seven criteria: a value is (1) chosen freely, (2) from among alternatives, (3) after careful consideration of the consequences of each alternative; and it is (4) prized and cherished, (5) willingly affirmed in public as well as (6) acted upon (7) repeatedly. Thus the three primary processes involved in valuing are *choosing, prizing,* and *acting.* To assist a person to develop values through the processes of choosing, prizing, and acting, one should (1) encourage the person to make choices and to make them freely, (2) help the person to discover and examine available alternatives when faced with choices, (3) help the person weigh alternatives thoughtfully and reflect upon the consequences of each, (4) encourage the person to consider what it is he or she prizes and cherishes, (5) give the person opportunities to make public affirmations of the choices made, (6) encourage the person to act and behave and live in accordance with the choices made, and (7) help the person to examine repeated behaviors and life patterns in relation to the choices made. These activities are quite different from an attempt to persuade someone to accept a predetermined set of values. (This difference, by the way, should help explain the opposition to the Values Clarification approach by persons who, and groups which, do have a set of values they are trying to promote among children.)

One does not aid a person to develop values by setting an example, persuading, limiting choices, inspiring, regulating, dogmatizing, or appealing to conscience, but by using the *clarifying response.* A clarifying response is one that stimulates persons to consider carefully the choices they have made, the thinking they have done about choosing, their behavior in light of choices, etc., thus gaining a clearer understanding of their own unique process. Some of the criteria for an effective clarifying response presented by Raths, Harmin, and Simon (1966) include (1) avoiding moralizing and criticizing; (2) putting the responsibility upon the person to personally decide what it is he or she wants; (3) allowing the person either to examine or not to examine (i.e., the clarifying response is permissive, not insistent); (4) providing a stimulating mood rather than trying to accomplish certain big goals; (5) individualizing and allowing personal reactions, etc. Clarifying responses are brief and spontaneous remarks made during a moment of face-to-face personal contact and are not "mechanical" procedures for use in an extended interview and apply identically to all persons. They are reactive, short, personalized comments that aid a person to examine choosing, prizing, and acting.

The Values Clarification group has, however, gone well beyond the clarifying response in suggesting procedures for classroom teachers. In *Values Clarification*, Simon and colleagues (1972) describe procedures that can be used for values clarification. Unfortunately, such procedures are often used as gimmicks by teachers who do not seem to really understand the theory behind Values Clarification procedures. Many of the procedures are in reality curricular units; another book (Harmin, et al., 1973) presents guidelines for use of subject matter to create opportunities for Values Clarification. Hence, what originated as *a description of how to respond* in a helpful way to another person's spontaneous expressions has developed into *a structured format for directing* persons into a consideration of their thoughts, plans, behavior, and commitments. The shift is akin to changing from stimulating repartee to organized questioning about topics the other party has not selected.

From the Values Clarification point of view, the competent valuer is one who (1) makes a point of choosing the values to which he or she gives commitment, (2) carefully analyzes all the implications of choices made, (3) has a "treasure chest" of cherished values, (4) designs actions and life patterns on the basis of the values chosen, and (5) willingly speaks to choices in public when it is appropriate to do so. Valuing competence is a matter of how one goes about making and acting upon those choices that give life direction, a matter of the attention and effort given to one's commitments. That such competence will lead to the selection of certain values is denied.

Because so many activities could be described as serving to clarify values, the research on the Values Clarification approach tends to be illustrative. Studies are undertaken using a specified procedure to illustrate Values Clarification rather than to contrast it with some alternative procedure. The findings based upon this specific procedure will then be considered supportive of the notion that Values Clarification does in fact lead to increased competence in valuing. For example, in a study conducted with college undergraduates who declared themselves undecided as to field of study, Ohlde and Vinitsky (1976) found that a seven-hour "values clarification workshop," designed to include strategies implementing all seven aspects of the valuing process, resulted in a significant increase in the correlation between (1) what a participant said were his or her values and (2) the values-based alternatives selected as potential vocational activities. In this instance the participants are assumed to have developed a closer relationship between what they say and what they do, such being one of the many possible indices of valuing competence derived from the Values Clarification approach. The statistically significant result is thus considered supportive of Values Clarification in general. A critical review of research on the effect of values clarification and moral development curricula upon school-age subjects has been written by Lockwood (1978).

THE SPECIFIC SKILLS IN VALUING

The Values Exploration Workshop (Simmons, 1978), designed as an opportunity for participants to explore themselves as valuers, consists of two four-hour sessions spaced a week apart and provides participants with the opportunity to:

1. rate where they are now and where they would like to be with regard to a variety of aspects of valuing, for example, "how accurately others perceive my values" or "how effective I am in resolving interpersonal value conflicts."
2. learn the ideas of some scholars of valuing, for example, Rokeach, Frankl, the Values Clarification group.
3. take an inventory of personal values, for example, the one-hundred item value survey mentioned previously.
4. identify their least-actualized values and plan some activities allowing those values to be expressed in action.
5. play a game called Val-You in which they roll a die to get a state-

ment stimulating a discussion about the relationship between their
behavior and their values.

6. conduct a joint interview to gain insight into sharing values and
   valuing perspectives.
7. reach some general conclusions about the nature of values and
   valuing.

The responses of participants to the last section of the workshop
included references to many skills involved in valuing. Over several
years the skills mentioned were added to a cumulating list, and a
conceptual analysis resulted in a semifinal list of twelve relatively non-
overlapping valuing skills.

It is now clear that these skills can be used as the basis for defining
valuing competence; that is, they are the attributes or components of
competent valuing. Competence in valuing may now be defined as skill
in —

1. stating specifically the values that are important in one's life.
2. describing how one's value system is organized and how flexible it
   is.
3. discussing with knowledge and intelligence the nature of the valuing process as well as taking positions on controversial issues about
   the nature of valuing.
4. recognizing how important one's values are to oneself and how
   willing one is to be open about them to others.
5. stating the reasons for commitment to each of one's values as well
   as how these values developed and are related to one another.
6. relating one's values to one's behavior and vice versa.
7. implementing and living by one's values as well as recognizing the
   specific difficulties one has in doing so.
8. keeping track of the changes in one's value system and creating
   processes to foster the implementation of new values.
9. identifying and coping with the conflicts among one's own values.
10. dealing with the role of one's values in the development, mainte-
    nance, and enhancement of one's interpersonal relationships.
11. learning the values of another person.
12. resolving interpersonal value conflicts and recognizing one's will-

ingness to compromise one's values in an interpersonal relationship.

The advantage of identifying the nature of valuing competence in the above way is the provision of criteria necessary for designing educational activities for fostering such competence.

SUMMARY

Skill in making correct value choices and judgments is to some educators simply the correct application of logic in the analysis of evidence. Three theoretical approaches to valuing competence, however, suggest that such competence involves more complex psychological processing than the adequate use of logic. Hartman proposed as the fundamental axiom of scientific axiology that "A thing is good when it fulfills the definition of its concept." Valuing competence involves skill in analyzing (1) the nature of a concept and (2) the degree of complexity in the fulfillment of a given concept by a given instance (thing, idea, or person). The greater the complexity, the greater the value. Kohlberg proposed that moral valuing skill is a product of principled moral judgment. Persons develop through an invariant sequence of stages, basing their judgments initially upon consequences, next upon community norms, and ultimately upon the general principle of justice. The central value in the resolution of interpersonal conflict is thus justice, and valuing competence consists of the level of application of this principle of justice in the resolution of those conflicts.

Dewey and the Values Clarification group view valuing as a process of moving from unsatisfactory to satisfactory conditions. The processes in evaluating one's current and future situation are choosing, prizing, and acting; and the clarifying response is recommended by the Values Clarification group as the best procedure for enhancing the development of choosing, prizing, and acting in an individual.

An alternative set of valuing skills derived from responses to the Values Exploration Workshop includes being able to state one's values, describe how one's behavior is related to one's values, and resolve interpersonal value conflicts. The advantage of defining valuing competence as a set of skills lies in the ready design of educational procedures to enhance such competence.

6.

Axiological Maturity
and Personal Development

Two tasks remain for this book. One is to tie the three aspects of valuing together in some integrated way for an understanding of the individual person, and the other is to provide the reader with some processes for relating personally to the ideas presented in the book. In this last chapter, then, there is an attempt to interrelate valuing content, fulfillment, and competence through the creation of a theoretical construct, *axiological maturity*. In addition, there is a presentation of a do-it-yourself Values Exploration "mini-workshop" for the reader's own use — a series of activities that could be used to build some of the skills mentioned in the last chapter.

The Possibility of Axiological Maturity

Assume you have volunteered to participate in a psychological research study. You turn up at the appointed time for the experiment and find yourself to be the last person to arrive. You move past the other four research subjects to the last chair at the table, facing the experimenter, who informs everyone that "You will be asked to make some perceptual judgments." A card is presented on which are two straight lines that to you are obviously unequal in length. When the first research subject says they are equal in length, you find yourself a bit puzzled but assume that visual weakness explains the incorrect judgment. However, when the second, third, and fourth subjects (who, unknown to you, are all in complicity with the experimenter) all state the lines are equal in length, you are faced with a dilemma. Should you now state your own perception, thereby admitting to the others and yourself that you are a true social deviant, or should you agree with the others and be comfortable through being in harmony with your fellow subjects? The other subjects are actually confederates of the researcher who has instructed them to respond in a way which will create (1) an agreement among them, and (2) a conflict in judgment between them and the lone research subject. This confrontation between personal judgment and social norm was designed by Asch (1956) as a procedure for studying conformity behavior and the conditions that influence it. This design has received so much commendation from social psychological researchers that it has become known as *the* conformity research paradigm. In one variant of this paradigm, the Crutchfield (1955) version, subjects sit in private booths and learn the responses of other subjects by watching a panel of lights. The advantage of this version is that the experimenter can control the apparent responses of the "other" subjects without anyone actually being a shill; i.e., all subjects can be presented with the same conformity dilemma at the same time.

The Crutchfield version of the conformity paradigm was used by Martin (1976) to study personal characteristics of those who stuck with their primary value in the face of conformity pressures. That is, when a subject was presented with a statement consistent with the terminal value he or she ranked highest on the Rokeach Value Survey and then learned that all other subjects disagreed with the statement, would the subject make a value-consistent judgment or a group-consistent judgment?

Martin was interested in a variable he called approval-seeking motivation and he predicted that persons low in approval-seeking motivation would make value-consistent judgments while persons high in approval-seeking motivation would make group-consistent judgments. In other words, value-consistent judgments would be reduced under conformity pressure conditions. The Martin study was in fact quite complex; and although the main hypothesis stated above was generally supported, one of the most striking results of the study was the set of values emphasized by the subjects with low approval-seeking motivation. Compared to approval seekers, such persons gave more weight to the terminal values of Equality, Freedom, and Wisdom and the instrumental values of being Broad-minded and being Courageous.

These findings by Martin seem crucial for several reasons. First, the values of Equality and Freedom have been credited by Rokeach (1973) as the source and foundation of sociopolitical ideology. Second, these two values form the basis for Ekhardt's (1972) compassion-compulsion dimension, which he believes should be promoted as the foundation for all personal and social living and organization. Third, freedom and equality are rephrasings (or near synonyms) of Kohlberg's (1969) two forms of justice, the distributive and the commutative, which must be reconciled at the highest level of moral reasoning. Fourth, persons high on the Identity Achievement Status Scale (Simmons, 1980), designed to assess the sense of personal identity defined by Erikson (1963), more often emphasize the *conjoint* importance of these two values than do persons scoring low on the scale.

When Martin's research findings are combined with the theoretical notions and research data of other scholars, the hypothesis emerges that the valuing of freedom and equality may be central to effective valuing. The implication of all of these various inputs is that the (possibly conjoint) valuing of freedom and equality is associated with compassionate sociopolitical ideologies, principled moral judgment, a high sense of personal identity, and a tendency to stand up for one's values in the face of pressures for conformity.

If it is accepted that those persons who are more committed to, and act upon, their values are more competent as valuers than persons who give in to pressures for conformity, we can derive the proposition that valuing competence is not independent of value system content but is an essential part of an integrated content-fulfillment-competence pattern. The identification of equality and freedom as *the* two values that may provide the clue to valuing competence and fulfillment suggests that research may have led us to Maslow's "naturalistically good values" or even to the two virtues that Plato maintained are the essence of the Good Man. The naming of the Good Values on the basis of research raises the issue of whether the "naturalistic fallacy" is being committed; hence, the reader is referred to Kohlberg's interesting paper (Kohlberg, 1971a) on how to commit the naturalistic fallacy and get away with it—whether psychology can tell philosophy the nature of correct ethical propositions.

This book began with a contrast between a more competent but less fulfilled young woman and a less competent but reasonably fulfilled young man. The comparison may have furthered the notion that competence and fulfillment are independent aspects of valuing. At this point we can now consider the proposition that under *ideal* conditions the more competent valuer will be more fulfilled than the less competent valuer. This requires the recognition that (1) from time to time specific situational constraints may hamper the fulfillment of even the most competent valuer, and (2) because the competent valuer has a more flexible approach to valuing, competence may be associated with fluctuations in level of fulfillment.

We thus find ourselves led to the proposal that there may be a general valuing characteristic, a dimension of individual differences, that we can label *axiological maturity*. Axiological maturity, when at its highest level, would be reflected in high valuing competence, high fulfillment of the valuer, and a high commitment to those values enhancing empathic and compassionate living—freedom and equality. The goal of values education would be to develop axiological maturity, and practices in values education would include efforts to aid each person to increase competence, fulfillment, and commitment to those values that enhance the quality of social life through balancing the rights of each person with the rights of others. Values education would then no longer be a singular process directed toward a single objective. Rather, it would become a complex process of developing an individual and would involve the enhancement of a variety of psychological skills.

PERSONAL DEVELOPMENT: CHOOSING, EXPRESSING, AND PLANNING

Consider that you are now about to take part in a workshop, to be guided through three sets of activities. The first activity provides you with an opportunity to choose from a long list of value statements those that you consider to be components in your value system and then to organize them into a visual display of your own system. During the second activity you will be challenged with a number of potential life crises and conflicts, daily routines, relationships, etc., and you will be called upon to think about the values you would use for coping with these challenges. The task invites you to examine how your values are related to your behavior. The third activity is an assignment requiring you to plan ways to deliberately and consciously act upon a few of your important-but-slighted values during the period of a week.

The first activity, *choosing and organizing,* is designed to facilitate your skills in stating your values and in describing how your value system is organized. The second activity, *expressing,* is designed to increase your skills in describing how your values are related to your behavior and vice versa. The third activity, *planning,* is designed to facilitate the building of skills in the implementation of values through practice in self-directed activities.

CHOOSING

Below you will find a list of value statements. As you read the list, draw a circle around those that are important to you, draw a line through those that you do not consider a part of your value system, put a check in front of those that you actively *reject.* Those values that are left over should be considered part of your value system, about which you have some feeling – but not much – or about which you have very mixed feelings, or about which you are puzzled or confused.

When you have finished responding to the prepared list, make a second list of values that are important to you but were not included in the prepared list, circling and checking as appropriate. Next write each statement that is included in your value system, that is, all those not lined out of the prepared list plus all those developed by you on the second list, on a one-by-three-inch slip of paper. Then begin sorting them out on a table or on the floor in whatever way makes the most sense to you. You may need a fair amount of space for this. It is also best to do the task only when you can proceed uninterruptedly for an hour or so, especially without kibitzing. For some people, this sorting out process involves ranking the statements from the most important to the least important (with ties acceptable). For others it means sorting their values into types or categories that go together because of their similarity or because of something they share. Still others may find that the sorting out results in the emergence of relationships among values; they may find that the value system is not organized as a hierarchy or as sets of categories but only as *patterns of relationships* among individual values. As the categories or patterns begin to emerge from your sorting, think of terms or labels that describe with a fair degree of accuracy the essence of the category or pattern.

When you have finished the sorting and labeling, take a piece of paper and record your placements, including the labels you have used to describe your categories. When you have finished this task, you should be in a good position to answer two questions when they are asked of you: (1) What are your values? and (2) What is the nature of your value system? In addition, you will have in your hands a concrete representation of your value system which you can use at some later time, after a resorting, to answer a third question: How have your values been changing?

One Hundred Possible Values

1. the opportunity to improve my standard of living.
2. owning my own land.
3. having modern conveniences like indoor plumbing and electricity.
4. having good health.
5. living to a happy old age.
6. having an adequate social security system.
7. being successful in my work.
8. having happy, healthy children.
9. being part of a happy family.
10. preserving social justice.
11. fighting for what I believe in.
12. a world without nations.

13. the state of ecstasy.
14. the state of tranquility.
15. an ever changing world.
16. a stable world.
17. a sense of heightened individuality.
18. the pleasure of being with others.
19. being the one who always brings about changes.
20. feeling the comfort of having others maintain a good world for me.
21. resisting the pressures to be or do something which is against my values.
22. developing new ways of living in the modern world.
23. maintaining the tried and true ways of living that have proven so good.
24. approaching the solution of social problems with unrestrained zeal.
25. resolving social disputes through calm diplomacy.
26. moderation in all moods.
27. a closeness with my own inner self.
28. being open and receptive to others.
29. enjoying sensual experiences with relish and abandonment.
30. merging myself with a companionable group.
31. continually and actively striving for some end.
32. experiencing an empathy for all ways of life.
33. floating along in a casual and carefree state of existence.
34. always being in control of my experiences.
35. overcoming or conquering some obstacle.
36. seeking adventure and excitement.
37. the joy of humility and cooperativeness that aids others to become more themselves.
38. the beauty of a work of art.
39. creating an object of beauty.
40. making a contribution to basic knowledge.
41. thinking ideas and enjoying thoughts.
42. the hope of being wealthy.

43. participating in the business life of the community.
44. being a part of political activities.
45. being in charge of the lives of others.
46. spending my time organizing and directing.
47. entertaining others.
48. spending my time at parties.
49. being recognized for my accomplishments.
50. the opportunity to become a celebrity.
51. being of service to others.
52. being as charitable as possible.
53. living a comfortable life.
54. leading a meaningful life.
55. living in a world at peace.
56. having equality among all men.
57. leading a life of freedom.
58. being a mature person.
59. living in a secure nation.
60. respecting others.
61. being respected by others.
62. achieving salvation.
63. achieving wisdom.
64. experiencing true friendship.
65. loving my parents.
66. becoming aware through rebellion.
67. developing and maintaining a career for myself.
68. establishing and maintaining a marriage and a family.
69. defending the oppressed.
70. maintaining a democratic society.
71. maintaining an efficient society.
72. avoiding an adherence to any ideology.
73. the joy of experiencing.
74. the technological marvels of our time.
75. controlling my own impulses so they don't get out of hand.
76. following the rules that I accept.
77. avoiding idleness.

78. avoiding anarchy through a strong central government.
79. achieving a sense of community or belonging together with all men.
80. being a decent, normal person.
81. developing myself into a more satisfying person.
82. feeling like a worthwhile person.
83. leading a disciplined life.
84. a world without fear.
85. accepting circumstances for what they are.
86. becoming aware of the potential for change around me.
87. developing or discovering means to change the world in which we live.
88. truth.
89. goodness.
90. order.
91. being unique.
92. simplicity.
93. justice.
94. playfulness.
95. a sense of everything being connected.
96. a sense of aliveness.
97. accepting the inevitable.
98. being victorious.
99. being myself
100. purity.

EXPRESSING

You may find the next activity simple, yet difficult. First, you will find a series of crises and challenges. Your task is to identify the value or values that *you* will apply to the solution of the crisis or challenge. (*Note:* Be sure not to decide the solution to the problem first. Identify the value(s) involved and *then* indicate to yourself how a solution derives from, or reflects, the value(s).)

Next, you will find the names of some relationships. State the name of the person who best qualifies for each relationship with you and identify the important value(s) involved in your relationship with each of these persons. (*Note:* Be sure to clearly describe to yourself how each of these values is expressed in the relationship.)

Third, you will find some issues. Decide which value is the most important one involved in that issue and then take a stand or personal position with regard to the issue. (*Note:* Be sure to state to yourself an opinion on an issue and clearly label the value involved in that issue. When you have done this, indicate to yourself how that value leads to your opinion. What actions follow from your opinions?)

Finally, you will find some daily routines. For each of these regular activities determine the value that organizes, or is reflected in, your pattern of behavior.

When you have finished the above tasks, you should be able to provide clear answers to the following questions: (1) How do your values serve as standards for guiding your behavior? and (2) Which of your values are influential in directing your behavior and forming your opinions?

CRISES AND CHALLENGES

1. A loved relative is seriously injured and asks you to relieve the suffering through a mercy killing.
2. You suddenly discover that you are popular because you never express an opinion that is controversial.
3. A friend offers to sneak you into a program that you could not otherwise attend.
4. You discover that you are in love with a person of another race.
5. A friend asks you to take a tough exam for him.
6. You are asked to provide birth control pills to a teenage friend whose parents are opposed to their use.
7. You discover a way to double your church offering through cheating on your income tax.
8. You reward people on the basis of their efforts rather than on the basis of their accomplishments, only to learn that they consider you wishy-washy because of this practice.
9. A friend confesses he is a homosexual and asks how he should tell his relatives.

10. You are asked to serve on a committee to censor pornographic materials.
11. Your steady is ill, so you go to a party alone, only to be asked (by a very attractive person) to sneak off to an apartment above.

Issues

1. Women's rights (politics).
2. What worship means to me (religion).
3. A proposal that able-bodied persons on welfare be required to work (economics).
4. The grading system (education).
5. Trial marriages (love, sex).
6. Radical protestors (law, rules, authority).
7. What I spend on others and what I spend on myself (material possessions).
8. Sterilization of the retarded (birth control).
9. What I'd do with a million dollars (personal wealth).
10. The future for mixed-race children (race).
11. Birth control pills (health).
12. What refreshes me most (leisure).

Relationships

1. father.
2. mother.
3. my favorite pet.
4. an aunt or uncle.
5. my worst enemy.
6. a boss or teacher.
7. my best friend.
8. a brother or sister.
9. a foreigner I know.
10. my children.
11. wife or husband (girlfriend or boyfriend).
12. strangers.
13. a cousin.
14. any relative you choose.
15. yourself.

Daily Activities

1. the way you eat.
2. your party behavior.
3. how you read the newspaper.
9. the programs you watch on TV.
10. the way you give presents.

4. how you spend your money. 11. your planned career.
5. the games you play. 12. your sleeping patterns.
6. your study habits. 13. how you care for your
7. the way you dress. belongings.
8. how you feel when you 14. the way you "goof off."
meet new people. 15. how you get upset and what
upsets you.

PLANNING

Select ten to fifteen of your most important values. Consider the extent to which each is openly and regularly expressed in your behavior and then rank the values from the one that is most clearly expressed to the one that is least clearly expressed. Select three values from the bottom of the list that, to you, appear to have some prospect for action; correspondingly, set aside any value that you have not acted upon because there is no real possibility for action.

Having selected three values, give yourself the following assignment: during each day of the next week, set aside a few moments when you can plan some way to express each of the three values during the day. *Note 1:* Do not plan out a whole week in advance; just plan for one day at a time. *Note 2:* Keep a short record of the extent to which you actually do express the value as planned, and of the consequences of your plans and actions.

This assignment may have the effect of making you aware that your activities are controlled by social commitments rather than being directed primarily by your own values. To express your own values with regularity, you may have to begin some reconciliation between your own desired inclinations and plans and the demands on you and expectations about you on the part of others. To be yourself may require the development of some skills in negotiation and diplomacy. Careful consideration of the long-range consequences to yourself and to others of going along with social expectations versus expressing your own values is a skill that can develop only with practice.

The planning exercise should help you to answer two questions about yourself as a valuer: (1) What sort of skills have I developed for designing ways of acting upon my values? and (2) How carefully do I consider the consequences of acting upon my values versus just going along with social expectations?

A FINAL QUESTION

This book has been about the "menus" created by various scholars to describe the "meal" we call valuing (and about a new menu that you could use to create for yourself more nourishing and exciting and tasty meals). These menus are efforts to attach words to ongoing processes that are not themselves really words: attempts to label and classify and measure the flow of living. Unfortunately for some persons in Western (occidental) society, the words and classifications and measurements may become more real than the processes and flow they are designed to describe. In *The Way of Zen*, Watts (1957) directs our attention to some of the notions of Eastern (oriental) society. By his measure, realizing the importance of certain goals in life, appreciating the fulfillment of a hope, and deciding that a certain course of action is the most correct are but ripples in the stream of life, which, when identified and labeled and measured, are already gone and hence no longer real. The effort to conceptualize as "thingness" that which is only process is a futile compulsion of Western thought, but its absurdity is recognized only when it is carried to extremes.

Suffice it to say that the author of this book hopes he recognizes a difference between a menu and a meal (and not just because eating the menu is not very tasty or nourishing). A more important hope is that reading this book as an introduction to the various contemporary menus about valuing will have led the reader to a clear understanding that valuing is other than and more than any of the menus presented. The book is, however, a very Western attempt to present those concepts about valuing that have led to labeling, classifying, and measuring. You, as reader, may now wish to ask yourself a further question. How will you pursue further understanding of human valuing?

REFERENCES

Allport, G. W.; Vernon, P. E.; and Lindzey, G. *Manual: A Study of Values*. 3d ed. Boston: Houghton Mifflin, 1960.

Asch, S. "Studies in Independence and Conformity: I. A Minority of One against a Unanimous Majority." *Psychological Monographs*, 1956, *70*(9), Whole No. 416.

Austin, J. J., and Van Arkel, C. *Muskegon County Jail Rehabilitation Program: An Evaluation*. Muskegon, Mich.: Muskegon Public Schools, 1973.

Blatt, M., and Kohlberg, L. "The Effects of Classroom Moral Discussion upon Children's Level of Moral Judgment." In *Recent Research in Moral Development*, edited by L. Kohlberg and E. Turiel. New York: Holt, Rinehart and Winston, 1973.

Blau, T. H. "Quality of Life, Social Indicators and Criteria of Change." *Professional Psychology*, 1977, *8*, 464–73.

Brogden, H. E. "The Primary Personal Values Measured by the Allport-Vernon Test." *Psychological Monographs*, 1952, *66* (16), Whole No. 348.

Cantril, H. *The "Why" of Man's Experience*. New York: Macmillan, 1952.

Cantril, H. *The Pattern of Human Concerns*. New Brunswick, N. J.: Rutgers University Press, 1965.

Crumbaugh, J. C. "Cross-Validation of Purpose-in-Life Test Based on Frankl's Concepts." *Journal of Individual Psychology*, 1968, *24*, 74–81.

Crumbaugh, J. C. "Frankl's Logotherapy: A New Orientation in Counseling." *Journal of Religion and Health*, 1971, *10*, 373–86.

Crumbaugh, J. C., and Maholik, L. T. "An Experimental Study in Existentialism: The Psychometric Approach to Frankl's Concept of Noogenic Neurosis." *Journal of Clinical Psychology*, 1964, *20*, 200–7.

Crumbaugh, J. C.; Raphael, M.; and Shrader, R. R. "Frankl's Will to Meaning in a Religious Order." *Journal of Clinical Psychology*, 1970, *26*, 206–7.

Crutchfield, R. S. "Conformity and Character." *American Psychologist*, 1955, *10*, 191–98.

Dandes, H. M. "Psychological Health and Teaching Effectiveness." *Journal of Teacher Education*, 1966, *17*, 301–6.

Dewey, J. "Theory of Valuation." In *International Encyclopedia of Unified Science*, vol. 2, no. 4, edited by O. Neurath. Chicago: University of Chicago Press, 1939.

107

Durkheim, Emile. *Moral Education: A Study in the Theory and Application of the Sociology of Education.* Translated by E. K. Wilson and H. Schnurer from the original 1925 version published posthumously in French. New York: Free Press, 1961.

Eckhardt, W. *Compassion: Toward a Science of Human Value.* Oakville, Ontario: Canadian Peace Research Institute, 1972.

Erikson, E. *Childhood and Society.* 2d ed. New York: Norton, 1963.

Feather, N. *Values in Education and Society.* New York: Free Press, 1975.

Findlay, J. N. *Axiological Ethics.* London: Macmillan, 1970.

Flacks, R. "The Liberated Generation: An Exploration of the Roots of Student Protest." *Journal of Social Issues,* 1967, *23,* 52–75.

Flanagan, J. C. "A Research Approach to Improving Our Quality of Life." *American Psychologist,* 1978, *33,* 138–47.

Frankl, V. *Man's Search for Meaning: An Introduction to Logotherapy.* Boston: Beacon Press, 1962.

Frankl, V. *The Doctor and the Soul: From Psychotherapy to Logotherapy.* 2d ed. New York: Knopf, 1965.

Gordon, L. V. "A Typological Assessment of 'A Study of Lives' by Q-methodology." *Journal of Social Psychology,* 1972, *66,* 55–67.

Gorlow, L., and Barocas, R. "Value Preferences and Interpersonal Behavior." *Journal of Social Psychology,* 1965, *66,* 271–80.

Gorlow, L., and Noll, G. A. "A Study of Empirically Derived Values." *Journal of Social Psychology,* 1967, *73,* 261–69.

Harmin, M., et al. *Clarifying Values through Subject Matter: Applications for the Classroom.* Minneapolis: Winston, 1973.

Hartman, R. S. "The Science of Value." In *New Knowledge in Human Values,* by A. H. Maslow. New York: Harper and Row, 1959.

Hartman, R. S. *The Structure of Value: Foundations of Scientific Axiology.* Carbondale and Edwardsville: Southern Illinois University Press, 1967.

Hartman, R. S. *The Hartman Value Profile: Manual of Interpretation.* Muskegon, Mich.: Research Concepts, 1973.

Hume, D. *An Inquiry concerning the Principles of Morals.* 1751. Reprint. New York: Liberal Arts Press, 1957.

Kilpatrick, F., and Cantril, H. "Self-anchoring Scales: A Measure of Individuals' Unique Reality Worlds." *Journal of Individual Psychology,* 1960, *16,* 158–73.

Kluckhohn, F. R., and Strodtbeck, F. *Variations in Value Orientations.* Evanston, Ill.: Row, Peterson, 1961.

Kohlberg, L. "The Development of Modes of Moral Thinking and Choice in the Years 10 to 16." Doctoral dissertation, University of Chicago, 1958.

Kohlberg, L. "Moral Development." *International Encyclopedia of Social Sciences.* New York: Crowell, Collier, and Macmillan, 1968.

Kohlberg, L. "Education for Justice: A Modern Statement of the Platonic View." In *Moral Education,* edited by R. Mosher. Cambridge, Mass.: Harvard University Press, 1969.

Kohlberg, L. "From Is to Ought: How to Commit the Naturalistic Fallacy and Get Away with It in the Study of Moral Development." In *Cognitive Development and Epistemology,* edited by T. Mischel. New York: Academic Press, 1971a.

Kohlberg, L. "Stages of Moral Development as a Basis for Moral Education." In *Moral Education: Interdisciplinary Approaches*, edited by C. M Beck, B. S. Crittenden, and E. V. Sullivan. Toronto: University of Toronto Press, 1971b.

Kohlberg, L. *Collected Papers on Moral Development and Moral Education.* Cambridge, Mass.: Center for Moral Education, Harvard University, 1973.

Lockwood, A. S. "The Effects of Values Clarification and Moral Development Curricula on School-age Subjects: A Critical Review of Recent Research." *Review of Educational Research*, 1978, *48*, 325–64.

Lurie, W. A. "A Study of Spranger's Value Types by the Method of Factor Analysis." *Journal of Social Psychology*, 1937, *8*, 17–37.

Martin, H. J. "Approval-Seeking Motivation: A Determinant of Conformity to Group Norms Inconsistent with Personal Values." Master's thesis, Oregon State University, 1976.

Maslow, A. *Toward a Psychology of Being.* 2d ed. New York: Van Nostrand, 1968.

Maslow, A. *The Farther Reaches of Human Nature.* New York: Viking, 1971.

Metcalf, L. E. *Values Education: Rationale, Strategies, and Procedures.* Washington, D. C.: National Council for the Social Studies, 1971.

Mezei, L. "Factorial Validity of the Kluckhohn and Strodtbeck Value Orientation Scale." *Journal of Social Psychology*, 1974, *92*, 145–46.

Mill, J. S. *Utilitarianism.* 1861. Reprint. Indianapolis: Bobbs Merrill, 1957.

Morris, C. *Paths of Life.* New York: Harper and Brothers, 1942.

Morris, C. *The Open Self.* New York: G. Braziller, 1948.

Morris, C. *Varieties of Human Value.* Chicago: University of Chicago Press, 1956.

Ohlde, C. D., and Vinitsky, M. H. "Effect of Values Clarification Workshop on Values Awareness." *Journal of Counseling Psychology*, 1976, *23*, 489–91.

Ornstein, R. E. *The Psychology of Consciousness.* San Francisco: Freeman, 1972.

Panowitsch, H. R. "Changes and Stability in the Defining Issues Test." Doctoral dissertation, University of Minnesota, 1975.

Papajohn, J., and Speigel, J. *Transactions in Families.* San Francisco: Jossey-Bass, 1975.

Pearson, P. R., and Sheffield, B. "Purpose-in-Life and the Eysenck Personality Inventory." *Journal of Clinical Psychology*, 1974, *30*, 562–64.

Piaget, J. *The Moral Judgment of the Child.* London: Routledge and Kegan Paul, 1932.

Porter, N., and Taylor, N. *A Handbook for Assessing Moral Reasoning.* Cambridge, Mass.: Center for Moral Education, Harvard University, 1973.

Raths, L. E.; Harmin M.; and Simon, S. *Values and Teaching.* Columbus, Ohio: Merrill, 1966.

Rest, J. R. "Manual for the Defining Issues Test." Unpublished manuscript, 1974. (Available from the author, 303 Burton Hall, University of Minnesota, Minneapolis, Minn. 55455.)

Rest, J. R. "The Research Base to the Cognitive Developmental Approach to Moral Education." In *Values and moral development*, edited by T. J. Hennessy. New York: Paulist Press, 1976.

Rest, J. R.; Cooper, D.; Coder, R.; Masanz, J.; and Anderson, D. "Judging the Important Issues in Moral Dilemmas—An Objective Test of Development." *Developmental Psychology*, 1974, *10*, 491–501.

Rest, J. R.; Davison, M. L.; and Robbins, S. "Age Trends in Judging. Moral Issues: A

Review of Cross-sectional, Longitudinal, and Sequential Studies of the Defining Issues Test." *Child Development,* 1978, *49,* 263–79.

Rokeach, M. *The Open and Closed Mind.* New York: Basic Books, 1960.

Rokeach, M. "Long-Range Experimental Modification of Values, Attitudes, and Behavior. *American Psychologist,* 1971, *26,* 453–59.

Rokeach, M. *The Nature of Human Values.* New York: Free Press, 1973.

Sahakian, W. S. *Systems of Ethics and Value Theory.* Totowa, N. J.: Littlefield Adams, 1968.

Sampson, E. E., editor. "Stirrings Out of Apathy: Student Activism and the Decade of Protest." *Journal of Social Issues,* 1967, *23*(3).

Schneider, M. "The 'Quality of Life' and Social Indicators Research." *Public Administration Review,* 1976, *36,* 297–305.

Shostrom, E. L. "A Test for the Measurement of Self-actualization." *Educational and Psychological Measurement,* 1965, *24,* 207–18.

Shostrom, E. L. *Manual: Personal Orientation Inventory.* San Diego: Educational and Industrial Testing Service, 1966.

Shostrom, E. L., and Knapp, R. R. "The Relationship of a Measure of Self-actualization (POI) to a Measure of Pathology (MMPI) and to Therapeutic Growth." *American Journal of Psychotherapy,* 1966, *20,* 193–202.

Simmons, D. D. "Development of an Objective Measure of Identity Achievement Status." *Journal of Projective Techniques and Personality Assessment,* 1970, *34,* 241–44.

Simmons, D. D. "Coming to Grips with Your Values: Materials for the Values Exploration Workshop." Corvallis, Ore.: Oregon State University Bookstore, 1977.

Simmons, D. D. *Values Exploration.* 2d ed. Corvallis, Ore.: Oregon State University Bookstore, 1978.

Simmons, D. D. "Identity Achievement and Axiological Maturity." Unpublished manuscript, 1980.

Simon, S. B.; Howe, L. W.; and Kirschenbaum, H. *Values Clarification: A Handbook of Practical Strategies for Teachers and Students.* New York: Hart, 1972.

Smith, A. "The Theory of Moral Sentiments." 1759. Reprint in *Adam Smith's Moral and Political Philosophy,* edited by H. Schneider. New York: Hafner, 1948.

Spranger, E. *Types of Men: The Psychology and Ethics of Personality.* Translated by P. J. W. Pigor from the 5th edition in German. Halle (Salle): Max Niemeyer Verlag, 1928.

Superka, D.; Ahrens, C.; Hedstrom, J. E.; Ford, L. J.; and Johnson, P. L. *Values Education Sourcebook.* Boulder, Colo.: Social Science Education Consortium, 1976.

Tanzer, D. "Natural Childbirth: Pain or Peak Experience." *Psychology Today,* October 1968, 16–21, 69.

Vernon, P. E., and Allport, G. W. "A Test for Personal Values." *Journal of Abnormal and Social Psychology,* 1931, *26,* 231–48.

Watts, A. W. *The Way of Zen.* New York: Pantheon, 1957.

INDEX